# HANDBOOK OF
# FINE BRANDIES

# HANDBOOK OF
# FINE BRANDIES

The Definitive Taster's Guide to the
World's Brandies

## GORDON BROWN

Macmillan Publishing Company
NEW YORK

Maxwell Macmillan International
NEW YORK  OXFORD  SINGAPORE  SYDNEY

Macmillan Publishing Company
866 Third Avenue, New York, NY 10022

Collier Macmillan Canada, Inc.
1200 Eglinton Avenue East, Suite 200
Don Mills, Ontario M3C 3N1

*Library of Congress Cataloging-in-Publication Data*

Brown, Gordon.
    Handbook of fine brandies: the definitive taster's
guide to the world's brandies/Gordon Brown.
        p.   cm.
    Includes bibliographical references and index.
    ISBN 0-02-517301-4
    1. Brandy.   I. Title.
TP599.B88 1990
641.2′53 — dc20    90-6288 CIP

First published in Great Britain by
Garamond Ltd, Publishers
Strode House
44-50 Osnaburgh Street
London NW1 3ND

Macmillan books are available at special discounts
for bulk purchases for sales promotions,
premiums, fund-raising, or educational use.
For details, contact:

Special Sales Director
Macmillan Publishing Company
866 Third Avenue
New York, NY 10022

10   9   8   7   6   5   4   3   2   1

Printed in Yugoslavia

# PREFACE

Wines and spirits mean different things to different people. Some like to stay with what they know; others like to experiment. The Italians and the Spanish will joyously try to market every new liqueur idea that comes to mind; the Americans and the Japanese will perfect a product, build the market around it and promote it. The French will establish a product and the market, and then legislate to the hilt to protect both, while the British approach is to take a quarter of a century to appraise a new generic direction before embracing it, and then wait 200 years before doing it again.

Brandy is drunk all around the world, but cognac has come to be the only world brandy. Why? Why do other countries' brandies not 'travel'? Have brandy-drinkers been too susceptible to the mystique of a spirit-drink from a country associated with so many other cultural and formative influences? Are we too ready to endorse something that is foreign and fashionable to the exclusion of all else just in case we do not fully understand it?

Brandies in other countries are also produced by traditional methods, to exacting standards and with great flair, forethought and innovation. The principal aims of this book are to help those interested to identify brandies, to define them and to be in a position to select effectively from the range on any shelf in the world where brandy is cherished and given its proper place.

To this end I have incorporated a succession of 'taste grids' which give a visual representation of the main characteristics of individual brandies. This format avoids the burden of often unctuous and repetitive adjectives which might otherwise be overworked in conveying impressions. These 'grids' may be used to assess single attributes — dryness, woodiness, fruitiness etc. — or overall style in a brandy, and also, very importantly, to locate other similar brandies that are unfamiliar to you.

Throughout the book, measurements have been given in both metric and Imperial units where necessary. Today, in the United States most spirits are sold in litres. For those unfamiliar with the metric system, 1 litre is roughly equivalent to 1 US quart or 1.75 UK pints.

With the information contained herein you can now compare directly your favourite cognac with others, or with an expensive Spanish brandy; an armagnac with a Californian brandy; a calvados with an applejack. The possibilities are endless.

Your very good health!

GORDON BROWN

# ACKNOWLEDGEMENTS

To all the brandymakers, proprietors, bouilleurs, families, enologists, association directors, managers, PR persons and assorted aides who took the time and often considerable trouble to help me — you know who you are and I offer you my warmest thanks for your generosity, good humour and understanding in everything you did.

Thanks, too, to Chris, Arthur and Tessa.

To Glen & the Kids. Remember Tuppence and Reuben? Good days.

# CONTENTS

## Der ytzt bedůckt

michnach vorhand: sein das
wir etwas herfurer theten vß
der werckstat d artzer: welche
ding des magēs/hertzē hirnes/der geist d
bnüsst vñ die krefftē beschieitē alsogantz/od
doch widerbrechtē/vñ ob doch flegma od
melancolya vberhand nem od der vnlust
vñ vodrutz entstōnde wie da wer weit hin
weg zů treiben vnnd zů helffen/Darumb
alle artzer on widerred hond verwilget dz
ist heilsamers sige/wā der tiriac od tria/
kers so zů enthalten vñ sterkēn alle geli

der vñ krefften/so ouch dynēt leiplichē
geisten vnd der vernūsst. Harumb d
tiriaco zům aller ersten sollen wir bruchē
ein halb quintlin oder ein dritten teil ein
quintlin das ist ein scrupel zwey mal al
wochen/des winters vnd im herbste/Als
im somer vnd glentzen einest oder einmā
in der wochen wie du wilt gar allein od
gefalt es dir zů kalten vnd fůchten zeitē
mit einem lutern claren süssen wein/abe
zů heissen vñ dürren zeitē Oorīß so d
natur oder das alter heisser ist/Mit vic
laten oder fūnktē

# INTRODUCTION

## BRANDY – WHAT IT IS, AND ISN'T

When we speak of fine brandy we almost always mean that noble digestive spirit that has been carefully distilled and matured in oak casks for long years. We also tend to assume that it is French. But, confusingly, the word 'brandy' has been broadened in its usage to embrace a wide range of spirit products which may have one or more fruit, nut or herb flavours added or enhanced in a number of different ways.

### SO WHAT IS BRANDY?

The term 'brandy' comes from the Dutch word *brandewijn*, meaning 'burnt wine', and refers to distillate derived from grape wine. The reason for its Dutch origin is that much of the early European distillation experimentation took place in the Netherlands in the Middle Ages and the Dutch were among the first Europeans to have a distillation vocabulary.

The principal brandy, then, is grape brandy, with French cognac so closely identified with the term that, even today, people are nonplussed when presented with French brandy that is not cognac or brandy that is not French – particularly if it is a fine brandy. As a direct result of its global success from about the middle of the 19th century, 'cognac' became the generic term internationally for better-quality brandy – *coñac* in Spain, *conhac* in Portugal, *konyak* in central Europe and so on.

Today, in order to protect the reputation of her famous brandy (and also her monopoly in a very important trade sector), France has repossessed the word and cognac must now come from Cognac in western France. Brandy from anywhere else – even in France – is disqualified from using the term no matter how fine its qualities, and brand names, like Lepanto in Spain, and company names, such as Asbach in Germany, must be impressed on the public consciousness by the brandy companies in order to register their association with fine brandy.

The regulations protecting cognac's name in French law relate to production method and geographic origin, not to quality *per se*. It has to be said that on the world's markets today there are

*The term 'brandy' comes from the Dutch 'brandewijn', meaning 'burnt wine' – much of the early European distillation took place in the Netherlands.*

cognacs of extremely modest quality and brandies of exceptionally high quality from other countries, yet people often pass the latter by owing to lack of information as to what exactly they are. What is special about cognac is the generally high merit of most of the brandy produced in its delimited zones and the excellence of the very best.

The dominance of cognac worldwide as the international brandy has meant that other countries' brandies, despite being extremely popular and commercially successful nationally, have been largely limited to their own home markets. Cultural links and affinities can certainly remedy this to a small degree, as, for example, in Spanish-speaking Mexico, where Domecq's Presidente, the world's top-selling brandy, sells over five million cases a year and another brand sells over two million cases, but few people are aware of the fine brandy that is produced in Spain, Italy, Portugal and Germany. As for most Americans and Australians, they are *au fait* with their own home-produced brandies yet know nothing about the small quantities of European brandies that have always been imported to these countries to serve minority communities.

Another type of brandy is made from the mass of skins, pips and other solids – the pomace – left behind after the grapes have been pressed. These brandies vary in their name according to where they are made – *grappa* in Italy, *marc* in France, *bagaceira* in Portugal and plain old pomace brandy in England. They tend to be much more of an acquired taste but their adherents are passionate about their merits.

Pomace brandies are made in many different qualities and volumes, from the rustic dozen litres emerging from an alarmingly vibrating and wheezing heirloom mini-still installed on the family half-acre to the rivers of aromatic spirit that rush from the serried stills of large Italian companies like Ramazzotti. Some types are made to mature in wood, others to drink young in order to enjoy the aroma and flavour of the grape. There is a wide variety of style and refinement to explore since the range of grapes used to make pomace brandies is both enormous and interesting. For example, Marc de Bourgogne is often made from grapes that grow on top Burgundy wine estates and you can buy Italian grappa made from Barolo and Barbaresco grapes.

*During the winter distillation period, the bouilleur's work is a kind of guard duty – the spirit's progress must be monitored at each critical point in the run.*

A third category of brandy comprises those made from fruits, such as kirsch (cherries), calvados (apples) and slivovic (plums) and so on. An important point here is that no flavourings or additives of any kind are involved in making these brandies; they are straight distillates from the fermented fruits.

To sum up the categories, we can make use of the terms that figure in French documentation: *eau-de-vie de vin* (grape brandy); *eau-de-vie de marc* (pomace brandy); and *eau-de-vie de fruits* (fruit brandy). This is where the line should be drawn in talking about brandy for the term to have any sense. Given that a grape is a fruit, brandies are straight distillates of fermented fruit (allowing for the addition of sugar, caramel and oak essences, which may be regarded as conditioners rather than flavouring elements) as opposed to whisky, vodka, schnapps etc. which are cereal-based. Most other spirits, apart from gin, rum and a few others, could be regarded as what are called 'liqueurs' in the UK and 'cordials' in the US – products like peach, cherry or apricot brandy, which are usually made with fruit or fruit essences added to silent spirit and sugar.

## A BRIEF HISTORY OF DISTILLATION

There is a ragbag of theories as to where and when distillation originated. Perhaps the earliest dated reference is 1000 BC in China regarding distillate from fermented rice, but the Ancient Egyptians, Greeks and Romans also knew about the process. Hippocrates and Pliny both wrote in some detail about distillation and spirits. Distillation went through several phases before it started to emerge as a means of producing a pleasurable drink. Alcohol's first uses were 'industrial', as a lamp-fuel, water-purifier, disinfectant and solvent in the making of perfumes and unguents.

Its name of *aqua vitae* – 'water of life' – initially had less to do with its restorative powers than with its preservative properties, since it was gained before people began to drink it. It preserved dead organic material placed in it and this led to the belief that the secret of life itself was somehow bound up with it. From that point a somewhat mystical aura built up around both the liquid and the science of making and using it.

There was a great deal of experimentation in and study of distillation and the properties of alcohol itself, largely done by Arab scholars during the ninth and tenth centuries. Their knowledge was disseminated throughout Europe from their colo-

*A hydrometer measures a spirit's alcohol content. Floating in a special chamber, it may be easily read by the distiller as spirit runs off the still.*

nial base in Spain. Many of the words associated with distillation are Arabic – for example, alcohol itself and alembic, a still.

Arnaldo de Villanova, claimed as a national by both Spain and France, extended the 'water of life' idea to therapeutic values that were to be gained from drinking well-made spirit, and a 13th-century Italian potentate, Ezzelino da Romano, interpreted this another way by plying guests with it in order to obtain valuable information from them which they might not otherwise have offered.

In medieval times, drinking alcohol in the form of medical potions and tonics made from herbs and roots macerated in alcohol was widespread, and everyone, even those who could not read or write, knew what *aqua vitae* was. The French equivalent was *eau de vie* and indeed Scotch and Irish whiskies in their respective branches of the Gaelic language – *uisge beatha* and *usque baugh* – translate the same idea.

By the 16th and 17th centuries trade in grape-distillates was well-established, with Jerez, Gascony and Charente supplying the northern European countries, and the city-states of Italy trading among themselves. In the same period colonists began taking distilling skills with them to North America and, later, to Australia.

Until the early 19th century distillation was always carried out in variations of the pot-still which had to be recharged after each individual operation. In 1827, Robert Stein, a forbear of the great Scotch whisky-distilling Haig family, invented and put into production a still which

11

*Accredited cognac is double-distilled over a naked flame.*

Other brandies are made without any specification whatsoever as to where the grapes are grown. In Spain, the majority of Jerez brandies used to be made from local grapes, but nowadays all of these go into the making of sherry wine and grapes from further afield in Spain are used.

In other countries such as Italy and Australia, the only geographic prescription is that the grapes be grown in the country itself. In California, brandy must be made from grapes grown within the state boundaries. Germany uses all its own grape-production for wine-making and brings in semi-fortified wines from Italy and France (including, it so happens, the Cognac area) to make its brandy.

### Grapes

Some brandies must be produced only from grapes named in the appropriate regulations, with options to include certain others, again specified, in minority proportions. The purpose of this is to standardize the broad generic style of the product

successfully distilled a continuous flow of fermented beer into good spirit. Stein's machine had been demonstrated before the Excise authorities at Wandsworth in London, and a Dublin Excise officer called Aeneas Coffey received details of the design and further improved it. Developments of the latter still have since spread around the world and formed the basis of continuous distillation, a process that is faster and cheaper than discontinuous distilling, but which refines spirit much more – a mixed blessing depending on the kind of distillate needed.

### Vineyard zones

Certain brandies are made according to very precise regulations and, in some cases, these include specifying where the grapes from which the distilling wine is made must be grown. This is because there are characteristics in the balance of the soil-types in which the vines are planted which have a direct bearing on how the grapes – and, hence, the wine – turn out.

Cognac's vineyards in the Charente districts of western France are probably the world's most specifically categorized brandy-production zones. They are divided into six different areas and ranked very broadly according to the chalk content in the soil of each. Armagnac, also in France, is divided into three separate zones, again based on the style of spirit that ultimately is made from grapes grown in each.

These details are not to do with high quality *per se*, but with the geographic origin and the taste/aroma profile of the different spirits which then go on to be blended.

*Regulations for cognac and armagnac grapes are strict.*

and make for ease in blending. Cognac and armagnac are subject to such regulations, the compulsory grapes being any one or more of Ugni Blanc, Folle Blanche and Colombard, but almost everywhere else brandy-makers choose the grapes themselves.

Experimentation goes on all the time in other countries, some using local grapes, others cognac grapes and still others both. A large proportion of the world's brandy requires only grapiness in aroma and flavour, and so is produced in continuous stills which do not retain the individuality of specific grape types. This gives brand-owners maximum freedom in choosing the house-style.

## Regulations

All countries have regulations relating to the production of brandy. For almost all of them it is principally a matter of ensuring minimum production standards in the name of public health and safety together with category definitions for the purpose of revenue-earning taxation. Extra details move into the area of shaping or confirming the nature of the product itself – usually in consultation with distillers' professional bodies and associations – in order to protect consumers in their expectation as to what it should be.

*The delimitation of cognac's production area in 1909 gave the appellation the characteristics of a trademark.*

## Fermentation

When grapes are pressed into juice, their yeasts – the dull smudges on their otherwise shiny skins – consume the sugar in their pulp, setting up the process of fermentation. Alcohol is produced as well as carbon dioxide gas, which is why there is so much froth present during that time (and it is also why people pass out if they put their heads into vats to have a good view of what is happening).

The wines produced for brandy-making around the world vary according to the style wanted. Light, elegant but austere brandy that has very long ageing potential derives from thin, acidic, low-strength wines that are pretty tough to drink, while smoother, more relaxed and gregarious brandy styles, whether light or fuller in body, emerge from balanced, complete wines that have 10–11% abv and are pleasant to drink.

## Distillation

All of the alcohol in a brandy originates in the fermentation of the fruit and it is then concentrated by the process of distillation. This simply means boiling the alcoholic vapours off the wine and collecting them as condensed liquid; if the process is repeated with the condensate, a strong spirit is produced that could be anything from 50% to 90% abv, depending on the equipment used. This is possible because alcohol boils at a lower temperature than water. In a distillation run, by the time the water is ready to boil all the alcohol has already done so, leaving most of the water behind.

This basic principle of distillation may be easily seen with a *pot-still*, which is filled with wine, boiled off, emptied of lees and water and then refilled in order to start the process again. Each batch is distilled twice in order to achieve the strength and concentration required. This traditional type of still, usually made of copper, gives a good combination of strength and flavouring elements, called congeners, in the resulting spirit.

The first part of the spirit to run off the still carries a high proportion of unpleasant impurities and is very strong. This is called the 'heads' and is channelled off for redistillation with the next loading. The good quality spirit, which now follows, is called the 'heart' or 'the middle cut' and is collected until its strength, which falls steadily throughout each boiling process, indicates that it is mainly water. When this point is reached, the supply from the still is cut off from the heart and the 'tails' are run to waste.

The procedure is more complicated in a *continuous*, or *coffey*, still which can distil a continuing flow of wine into spirit, is very efficient and can distil up to a very high strength. When this is done congeners are lost and the spirit produced is neutral. It is also, however, very smooth in texture and finish when reduced to bottling strength and thus has definite commercial value in the production of light, blended brandies.

*No nails or glues are used in the cask. To ensure a watertight, exact-fit the tapered staves are worked over a flame.*

## Maturation

In many locations throughout Europe, the discovery was independently made many times over that *aqua vitae* improved after being stored over a period of time in wooden containers. Oak forests were widespread and plentiful so oak wood figured strongly as a construction material for barrels, and the benefits it endowed on what, long ago, must have been rather harsh and elemental distillates would have been readily noticed. Other woods are now also used and, indeed, specified for particular brandies in different locations; chestnut, cherry, acacia, beech, even ash, and others do a similar job in different ways.

*An oak cask will impart colour and flavour to the spirit, removing it's fieriness and allowing it to mature by oxidation.*

Oak casks impart colour and an attractive, smoky, vanilla flavour to clear spirit, the main transfer substances being tannin and vanillin. They also temper the spirit, taking the fieriness from it and allowing it to mature by oxidation through the wood's pores. New wood tends to be used on raw, new spirit in order to have most influence when most needed. Subsequent to this, gentler, slightly spent woods are used according to the effect desired on older, partly-mellowed brandies. New wood is not used on older spirits because they would be overwhelmed with oaky aroma and flavour.

Maturation is normally a matter of storing brandy carefully and leaving time to do gradually what is expected of it. However, in Spain the brandy-makers use what they call the 'dynamic ageing' of the *solera* system which has the remarkable effect of accelerating maturation through careful blending (see page 69).

A controversial element in fine brandy is *boisé*, a process whereby woody characteristics are leached from oak chips by infusing them in hot water and brandy. The liquid is then added in small proportions to maturing brandy in cask. A weak solution will merely adjust the tannin-level of a brandy, a procedure which apparently helps maintain consistency of style; the trouble is that a strong solution will add aroma, lending the impression that the brandy has undergone more cask-ageing than is actually the case.

*Boisé* is quite legal and has been used for hundreds of years. It is an optional part of the production of cognac, including, surprisingly, the expensive, higher-quality designations like XO. There is no question of its being used secretively, but it must raise doubts in consumers' minds as to the genuineness of those lovely mature, woody aromas they savour so much and for which, of course, they pay when they buy more expensive brandies. Perhaps it is time the practice was stopped or at least standardized.

## Label information

All countries have regulations regarding what may and may not appear on the labels of brandy bottles. Mandatory information has to be clearly stated and often in print of specified dimensions so that it may not be hidden in a corner of a back-label. The United States pays particular attention to elements of ingredient-listing so that consumers are not unwittingly absorbing substances that they would rather avoid.

*Even cognacs from an individual estate will be blended from the production of several years, and those from a single harvest will be a blend of a number of vineyards.*

In some countries minimum requirements might be very basic, giving information about where the brandy was made, the bottle-fill, the generic name of the product, the producer and/or bottler and an indication of the brandy's strength. Greater detail could include the appellation and sub-zone where relevant, vineyard or property name, ageing details and so on.

Terms which mislead regarding the origin, style or quality of brandies – e.g. 'cognac-style brandy' or 'made from cognac grapes' – are forbidden in most countries but although descriptions like VSOP, Extra etc. have specific meaning in France,

they are widely used elsewhere in purely cosmetic vein.

While label information will normally be accurate and legal in most markets, certain terms have to be read in conjunction with local regulations to know exactly what they mean. Depending upon the origin of a brandy, 'blended' on a label can mean a mix of spirit from two different districts, or regions, or countries; or different types of spirit, or different ages of spirit. On the whole, if label data is informative in a factual way and understated, rather than fanciful or effusive, the product is probably valid and reliable.

15

# FRANCE

One particular French brandy – cognac – has so gripped the imagination of the world that sight has been lost of the fact that it is only one of a number of brandies of different preparation that are produced in France. No doubt, many people reason that if you have access to cognac why bother with any other brandy? This line of reasoning, however, would make little sense to any self-respecting Alsacien, Gascon or Norman, all of whom may well drink cognac, but probably only as second choice to their own local spirit.

France has many regions that produce wines in their own individual styles, from different grapes and according to different traditions, so that each is almost like a separate country. Each of these 'countries' – plus one which grows no grapes, and hence makes no wine – produces brandy and, although most of these brandies only have any significance in their own locale, some are important enough to have wider distribution.

Grape brandies are produced in most, but not all, of these regions, cognac being, of course, the best known. South of Bordeaux in France's south-west corner lies the region of Armagnac which, like Cognac, gives its name to a fine grape brandy which has been in production for longer than its more famous counterpart. It is produced from the same grapes, but using a different type of still, and a lower distillation strength gives it a fuller, rounder character.

Bordeaux, Burgundy, Côtes du Rhône, Champagne and other wine areas produce their own grape brandies called 'fines'; many produce a pomace brandy called 'marc' as well as, or instead of, a fine. Some areas prefer to make brandies from other fruit. Alsace is famous for an extraordinary range of eaux-de-vie from pears, different types of plum, raspberries and cherries while the marc from their famous Gewürztraminer grape takes a back seat.

Brandies from apples – usually called 'cider brandies' – are produced in three regions, only one

*Many regions in France produce wines in their own individual styles, from different grapes and according to local traditions.*

17

of which also has vineyards. The most famous – Calvados, from Normandy – is double-distilled in pot-stills.

All of the above brandies have their own set of regulations governing how they are produced but there is a further, rather mysterious, category – the grape brandy of no fixed abode. These are well turned out bottles with a high profile on store shelves but it is almost impossible to obtain any detailed information about them. They go through some of the blending routines of the regulated brandies and are prepared from grape distillate deriving from a number of different areas in France. They sell well and some brands are quite important.

The problem is that silent (neutral) spirit is probably also used in the blending process and this makes their manufacturers very shy about vaunting their pedigree. This is a shame because their flavours are very carefully constructed and some of them emerge in better shape than many three-star cognacs.

Contrary to general impressions, these brandies are not harsh and fiery, but soft, grapey and quite pleasant. They usually project a brand name very strongly and may describe themselves on a label only as French Brandy.

## GRAPE BRANDY – COGNAC

Cognac brandy takes its name from the town and region of the same name in western France. So famous is this name that it has totally confused people around the world regarding brandy and, more particularly, brandy from France. Is all brandy cognac? Is all French brandy cognac? Is armagnac also cognac? Is all cognac French brandy?

Only grape brandy produced from vines grown in an officially-designated area of the Cognac region may correctly be called cognac. The area lies across the two Charente *départements* of France, from east of Angoulême to the Atlantic coast on the north bank of the Gironde estuary. Cognac may also be called '*eau-de-vie des Charentes*' but no-one opts for this alternative.

Cognac sells 126 million bottles around the world every year in 171 markets; the top importers are the USA (28 million bottles), the UK (17 million), Japan (12½ million) and West Germany (11 million). With the exception of West Ger-

*The French champagnes are rolling pasturelands which overlie a unique form of geological stratum to which they have given their name – Campanian chalk.*

many, each of these countries consumes more cognac than do the French themselves at home, and while the Far Eastern countries have the highest consumption per capita of the most expensive quality cognacs, the Irish have, quite simply, the highest consumption per capita.

## The countryside

The Cognac countryside is pastoral, gentle and restful, with woodland dotting the stretches of hillocky fields that carry cereal crops, meadows and, of course, vineyards. Grand houses inside their walls and clumps of trees, churches and hamlets, almost all of a grey stone that looks its best in sunlight, repeat endlessly into the distance.

Village main streets are usually quiet, if not deserted, because life is lived behind gates and doors in the Charentes.

A walk down a cobbled main street will reveal centuries of decay and rustic repair in the continuous walling, but all of the sun-bleached wooden doors have padlocks on them and behind most are dark, sometimes damp, storage nooks stuffed with casks of cognac.

## History

The ancient peoples of France, the Gauls, established agriculture in the region and later the Romans brought the vine when their armies occupied the whole of what is now France. Although the English had an early interest in the Charentes and Bordeaux regions through the marriage of King Henry II to Eleanor of Aquitaine in 1152 – an event which helped form English drinking tastes for centuries to come – it was the Dutch who did much to shape the development of brandy-distilling around Cognac.

The Dutch traded along the Atlantic coast for salt and wine, the latter to drink in the normal way but also 'to burn'. They had distillation skills and brandewijn – 'burnt wine' – was the name they gave to the eaux-de-vie they produced from the wine they took back home. As burnt wine grew in popularity, it made sense to do the distillation in situ and substantially reduce the transportation volume, since 1 litre (1 quart) of cognac represents 10 litres of wine.

Distillation is thought to have begun in the area around 1530 but was not widespread until just under a century later. The 'pot charentais' (the pot-still used in Cognac to this day) was designed by the Dutch so that the Cognaçais could produce the kind of spirit the former wanted.

The brandy was single-distilled until the end of the 16th century, when a French nobleman is said to have discovered the improved refinement of a second distillation – the bonne chauffe. Ageing the brandy in storage casks, which happened to be of oak, caught on early in the 17th century and it is possible that this was a direct result of the distillers having less frequent trading contacts during wars. Casks of spirit would have to have been stored for long periods, even several years, before a ship might call and the new mellowness, aroma and colour would certainly have been noticed.

Augier, the oldest firm surviving today, was founded in 1643 but now is effectively nothing more than an ornament in the Seagram display cabinet. In the late 1840s Denis-Mounié and Jules Robin were the first companies to sell cognac in bottle and by the 1860s it was exported all round the world, becoming the most fashionable drink of its time.

Yet while all this success was building, a singular catastrophe was forming. A plant louse called phylloxera was accidentally introduced to Europe from America on a vine leaf and it spread throughout the continental vineyards, reaching Cognac in 1872. Phylloxera attacks vine-roots and within eight years the vineyards were totally blighted.

The solution was to graft all vines on to American rootstocks which were immune to phylloxera but it took 25 years to discover this, effect the replanting and get back into production. It also meant a change in the principal grape-type used.

The aromatic, acidic Folle Blanche had formerly been the first choice but it proved difficult to graft and was replaced by the Ugni Blanc, which gave a similar style of wine but which had less to offer in terms of aroma. Meanwhile, Scotch whisky had filled the void left by the sudden disappearance of cognac.

Once the Cognac vineyards were back into production cognac recovered its market position and in 1909 the land-zones within which grape-growing for the production of cognac brandy was sanctioned were officially delimited and its name was given the protection of law.

Trade flourished throughout the 20th century, with occasional problems like prohibition in the US, two world wars and overambition leading to overproduction in the 1970s. Much of the old cognac around today survives thanks to the officer in charge of the German forces that occupied the town of Cognac during the last war. He had gone to school there as a member of the family that ran the famous firm of Meukow and he was able to protect the brandy stocks from destruction or consumption. They were further saved when, instead of surrendering substantial amounts of valuable brandy requisitioned for sending to Germany, the merchants handed over spirit distilled from root vegetables.

### The brandy

Cognac is a light- to medium-bodied brandy, mainly dry, often austerely so, with the strength and warmth to be found in other brandies. When mature it attains great delicacy and fragrance with the elements of violets, wood, grapiness and slight nuttiness presenting themselves persistently but in a very understated way.

It is a subtle and gently lengthy brandy when at its best, with concentration despite its lightness. Very old cognacs develop considerable complexity and a distinctive, pleasantly decayed flavour called 'rancio', well described by Bernard Hine as slightly musty walnuts. Good cognac's capacity to balance its characteristics gives it great elegance.

Unlike great wines and malt whiskies, cognacs from single properties and/or single vintages are not necessarily a wonderful prize. Blending actually enhances cognac because it combines complementary distillates and enables it to attain a level of balance rarely offered by one estate or one summer. Even cognacs from a sole estate will be blended from the production of several years, and those from a single harvest will be a blend of a number of vineyards. Specific vintage years may not be declared on labels, although there is talk of restoring this practice in the future with the help of carbon 14 dating techniques to prove dates are as claimed.

*The oak wood imparts colour, aroma and flavour.*

### Vineyard zones

Many of the text-books describe cognac's accredited growing area as being 'strictly' delimited but this gives the impression of total and fierce adherence to matters of quality. 'Precisely' would serve better because the peripheral zones do not produce high-quality spirit and not all of the permitted growing area is even taken up for vine-production. Where utilized, the poorer soils yield brandy mainly for preserved fruit-bottling and local sale.

Broadly speaking, the chalkier the soil, the better the cognac that eventually derives from it. The champagnes of the French countryside are rolling pasturelands which overlie a unique form of chalk and they have given their name in geology to Campanian chalk as well as to famous French sparkling wine and fine brandy.

The best production zones are the chalky Grande Champagne and Petite Champagne, both of them yielding delicate and very subtle cognacs which may, but do not necessarily, stand well on their own. Even from the best areas, the distillation wine rarely renders the required balance that adroit blending – the cornerstone skill in producing fine cognac – achieves, and brandies from each of these two areas are normally blended.

By combining brandies from different properties and different years, it is possible to create excellent balance which brings out the finesse of the zone styles.

Grande Champagne brandies have been known to improve in cask for up to 100 years, although most long-lived treasures are transferred to large glass demijohn jars after 60 years to avoid their becoming too woody in flavour and aroma.

Fine Champagne is not a zone; its presence on a label indicates a cognac made from grapes grown in both of the above denominations with at least 50% coming from Grande Champagne. Rémy Martin were the first to specialize in this style of blend, but quality can vary according to whether young or more mature cognacs are used.

This aspect of blending boosts the importance of the next category, the Borderies, where there is intermittent woodland among the meadow-crowned chalk. Bottlings exclusively of Borderies cognac are prized by those who enjoy brandy with a more positively-stated flavour.

There are almost a million acres of Fins Bois, a production area whose name acknowledges the substantial woodland presence in its less chalky, more predominantly arable soil environment.

*By combining brandies with different properties from various years, it is possible to create a correct balance which brings out the finesse of the zone styles.*

Fins Bois spirit matures faster and its abundance and its usefulness in blending ensure continuing brisk demand from the high-volume firms for their middle-range brands. About 40% of cognac brandy's volume derives from this sector. Some brandies exclusively from Fins Bois vines are produced and they are excellent, usually a little fuller-flavoured but still showing class and balance.

Bons Bois wines sell at just over 60% of the top grade prices but, in brandy terms, it is hard to make anything special out of them. There is very little chalk in the soil and much of the spirity and blowsy brandy produced from here goes into the cheapest cognacs used 'medicinally' or for mixing with ginger ale. The top brand-owning firms tend not to buy these cheaper wines, preferring to find all their blending requirements within the top four categories.

The Bois Ordinaires are very ordinary indeed and very little, if any, wine is made for the main cognac blending trade. Wine prices at just over half the top level are quoted but not much changes hands.

### Grapes

The Ugni Blanc grape is used for producing 90% of the white wine from which cognac brandy is made. Its wine is thin, acidic and low in alcohol – perfect for distilling the style of brandy cognac represents. Some growers lovingly struggle to produce the old Folle Blanche despite the difficulties involved and some Colombard is also grown, but four other permitted varieties are rarely seen now.

Its relatively trouble-free cultivation makes the Ugni Blanc popular among growers, but another reason for its dominance is that everyone wants to produce spirit in the same general style so as to make it easy to sell. No one wants to be out of line or too individualistic; leave all that to the blenders if they want to do something different. The vines have a lifespan of about 35 years, after which they are replaced by new vines which do not produce fruit until their fourth year.

### Regulations

The delimitation of Cognac's production area in 1909 effectively gave the *appellation* (its official registered name) the characteristics of a trademark which is recognized by law in the member-states of the European Community and by negotiation and representation elsewhere. The separate vineyard

*The alambic charentais is a beautiful piece of apparatus, with its slightly mysterious-looking, rounded, gleaming beaten copper metal set into brick housings.*

areas, or *crus*, are also part of that appellation so that 'Grande Champagne' printed on a label has to mean what it says. Brandies produced from individual crus are widely available and indicate a better brandy of a particular style. It is rare to see this done below the level of Fins Bois and illegal below that of Bons Bois.

A further decree in 1936 made the traditional methods and customary practices used in producing cognac mandatory so that no one could do anything radically different and still call his product cognac. This meant that viticulture, viniculture, distillation – including exclusivity of the Charentais pot-still – ageing in oak and other matters were all standardized to maintain the general style and character of cognac brandy.

## Distillation

Cognac must be double-distilled in a pot-still heated by a naked flame, according to the 'traditional Charentais method', to a maximum average strength of 72% abv and in practice no lower than 60% abv. The Charentais pot-still was originally designed by the Dutch in the 17th century when demand in the Netherlands for Charente brandy began to increase. It is essentially a copper kettle (the *chaudière*), a vaporizing bell (the *chapiteau*) and a condensing pipe (the *serpentin*) which coils

down through a vat of cold water to run the spirit into a collecting vessel.

It is a beautiful piece of apparatus, with its slightly mysterious-looking, rounded, gleaming, beaten-copper metal set into red-brick housings, and often rendered more intriguing by a bulbous wine-heater (a *chauffe-vin*) in the centre. This last is shaped like an upturned still and is the feed vessel for the wine that goes into the still itself. By routing the hot vapour pipe from the chapiteau through its middle, the wine is preheated.

These Charentais stills are always made of copper because it removes unwanted sulphides and is also resistant to acid.

The first distillation run produces the *brouillis*, a weak spirit of 30% abv; the second distillation – the *bonne chauffe* – is limited to 25-hectolitre batches of brouillis and this time it is cognac spirit that drips from the condenser pipe. Each run takes 12 hours. ('Distil' derives from the Latin words '*de*' and '*stillare*', to drip down.)

The spirit that is collected is a 'middle cut'. The high-strength initial volume (the heads) is foul and is set aside for redistilling and the same happens with the final part (the tails).

Cognac is best made from the freshest possible wine and distillation must take place before 31 March following the vintage five months earlier or the right to use the cognac appellation is forfeit. Such a disqualification would effectively render the spirit worthless, so it is a deadline everyone meets. Until recently there was the option to lose a year's ageing credit by registering the distillate after the following vintage, but this is no longer allowed.

Across the two Charentes *départements* there are thousands of one-man band distilling operations, single stills that turn out spirit for a grower's own wine or under contract for others. Most of these *bouilleurs* are families who have been distilling for the same large cognac firms for many generations and in the same location. They do well out of their profession but live unostentatious, even secluded, lives. Often the only clue to their comfortable status is the BMW or Mercedes that you see crouched at the back of the ancient yard by the stillhouse.

They work very hard and to a strict routine, but many confess to looking forward to the three-month winter distillation period when they sit snug and warm in the stillroom playing cards and talking endlessly with their cronies.

During these 12 or so weeks their work is a kind of guard duty, mostly involving monitoring the distillation at critical points in each run. There is always a bed or a couch and a table in the stillroom, since life is lived continuously alongside the stills at this time. At one time a candle used to be fixed on top of the swan-neck pipe (the *col de cygne*) that leads from the chaudière so that when the metal heated up from the vapours boiling off, the wax would melt and the candle would fall noisily into a box below to wake the distiller if he were asleep.

## Maturation

The spirit that comes off the still is colourless, but carries the aroma and message of the grapes from which the wine was made. These attributes are augmented during the years of ageing in oak casks that follow, when amber colour, aroma and flavour pass into the spirit from the lignin, vanillin and tannins in the oak wood.

The oak barrels are vitally important to proper development of cognac so many firms have their own cooper and some of the bigger ones their own cask factory. Hennessy who are a very large firm, recently bought their own forest.

Young cognac goes into new wood because both need tempering in their raw, upstart state, so maturation and mellowing applies both to cognac and cask. Once they have taken the fire out of each other they separate to take on different roles elsewhere, the cognac perhaps to be combined with others to start creating a final blend, and the cask to receive a partly-formed spirit that needs its gentler, less strident influence.

Cognac was traditionally aged in oak from the Limousin forests east of the town but this source is now greatly depleted – not surprisingly, since each 150-year-old tree only yields eight planks of the quality required. Oak is now used from Tronçais, a forest further afield that was first planted with the more sinister aims of furnishing wood to build a French fleet to sail against the English.

The wood must be left to mature after felling. It is stacked outdoors for five years to season before being split – not sawn – by a cooper to make cask staves. No nails or glue are used, the cask being shaped and held together by metal bands. In order to distract the attention of woodworm from the oak, each cask is also girt with thin hoops of chestnut wood, which they apparently prefer.

*Poorer vines yield brandy mainly for preserving fruit.*

23

Maturing cognac can lose as much as 3% per year of its volume by evaporation through the pores of the cask. This is the 'angels' share', the equivalent of 20 million bottles of brandy every year that goes into the atmosphere and blackens the walls and ceilings of the storage buildings.

This regular loss has to be made good by topping up the casks frequently, ideally with the same brandy. If the lost volume is not restored, the brandy will oxidize too rapidly. Alcoholic strength also reduces during maturation.

Cognac ages positively in wood for up to about 60 years. Beyond this, the oak aroma would overpower the other taste elements so it is usually transferred to large glass demijohns, if it is to be stored further, and development ceases.

When the ageing and blending are complete, the strength of each batch of brandy is reduced to 40 or 43% abv with *vieux faibles*, a weak solution of cognac and distilled water which merges more easily with the mature spirit. This is one of the last operations prior to bottling but, in order to give the batch time to marry, the time taken to carry out the strength-reduction can be five years.

Cognac, like brandies elsewhere, makes use of caramel for colour-control and cane sugar syrup (maximum dose of 2%) to soften excessive bite in the finish, and it is at this stage that this is done.

A permitted additive to cognac that often raises eyebrows is essence of oak chips, which, if used, is added in a spirit's early years. It is meant to give the impression of age through the oaky aroma that it fosters. This would otherwise only come from years spent in a cask – and even then the cask would still have plenty of influence to impart.

Oak essence is added to brandies just about everywhere they are produced, but it is not the kind of feature that appears in promotional literature. It usually only applies to the cheapest brands; it is regarded as corner-cutting by purists and is not encouraged. It is therefore somewhat surprising that it is allowed in cognac.

With cognac, oak chips essence (*le boisé*) is used not only to try to retrieve irredeemably rough adolescent brandies; it is added to cognac of VSOP and higher qualities where one would not expect shortcuts of any kind. And, since it is added early in a brandy's life, its use seems to be part of a spirit's planned development instead of a later corrective adjustment.

No indication is shown on bottle labels and, given the cognac authorities' consciousness of their product's image, it seems strange the practice is still permitted.

*Wood must be left to mature after felling. It is stacked outdoors for 5 years to season before being split into staves.*

## Label information

Most markets, including the USA and the European Community, allow cognac to go on sale when it is two years old and even in the British Isles, where a three-year minimum age has long been in force, the lower norm may be adopted if new European Community legislation goes through. Several Far Eastern Countries still require the extra year.

| | Legal min. age | Usual min. age | Main parameters |
|---|---|---|---|
| VS/THREE STAR | 2 yrs | 3 yrs | 3–7 yrs |
| VSOP/VO/RESERVE | 4 yrs | 5 yrs | 5–15 yrs |
| NAPOLEON | 6 yrs | 6/7 yrs | 7–15 yrs |
| XO/EXTRA | 6 yrs | 6/7 yrs | 20 yrs plus |
| VIEILLE RESERVE/ VIEUX | 6 yrs | 6/7 yrs | 7–40 yrs |

All ages refer to the youngest cognacs in the blend. The Bureau National Interprofessionel du Cognac guarantees the age of cognacs only up to six years.

Vintage cognacs have not been permitted in France due to the obvious problems involved in

*Prior to bottling, the spirit is inspected for impurities.*

monitoring topping up of casks in thousands of cellars throughout the region. However, a special form of vintage cognac does still legally exist – that of early-landed.

If a cognac, less than six years old and thus guaranteed by the BNIC as above, is exported to the UK and stored 'in bond' (allowing no physical access whatsoever by the public) with Her Majesty's Customs and Excise, the combined documentation guarantees the vintage and age when the duty is paid and the casks collected.

Cognac that ages in the damp UK emerges softer and more whispery than the equivalent in drier France and 'early-landed' should mean cognac from a cask that was imported very young and bottled much later, say 20 years, after a 'British' ageing. If one buys early-landed cognac, tacit in that purchase is the expectation of this late bottling since it would not make sense to import a young cognac, bottle it (thus arresting its development totally) and hang on to it for 20 years before trying to sell it. Hence the full term 'early-landed late-bottled'.

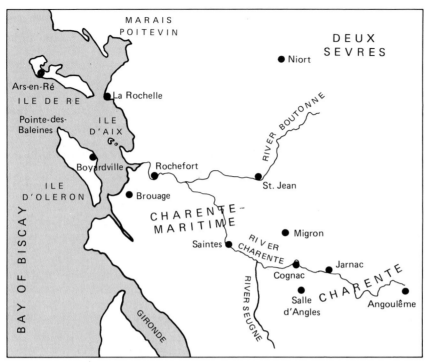

*The vineyards of Cognac lie across the départements of Charente and Charente-Maritime in west central France.*

## Places to visit

The well-known cognac houses are easy to visit but not all are located in the town of Cognac. Those that are include Hennessy, Martell, Otard and Camus; Hine and Courvoisier are in Jarnac, and Bisquit are at Lignières, 20 km (12½ miles) from Cognac.

PRODUCE OF FRANCE

# CHATEAU DE BRIVES

## COGNAC

APPELLATION
**PETITE CHAMPAGNE**
CONTROLEE

BRIVES SUR CHARENTE 17800 PONS

*Château de Brives, a 15-year-old single property cognac.*

Visits may also be arranged to the premises of producers of pineau des Charentes, a blend of cognac and unfermented grape juice. Do taste some during your visit. Good pineau is intensely grapey in flavour, full-bodied and sweet, so it is usually served very cold.

There are cognac museums in Cognac town, Salles d'Angle and Migron.

Cognac has another claim to fame which has nothing to do with brandy. Its annual film festival in April specializes in the detective genre and is regarded as sufficiently important to be part of the international film festival circuit.

Near Cognac, there is a first-century Gallo-Roman theatre at Les Bouchauds which held an audience of 10,000, and the sanctuary there is currently being excavated.

If you like châteaux, there is a stunning succession of them on the Saintonge 'Treasures Route'. The best-known is La Roche-Courbon, a real Sleeping Beauty castle with baluster terraces, sculpted gardens, Louis XIII-style rooms and much more. To the west of La Roche-Courban lies a stretch of the distinctive salt marshes particular to the area. Brouage is a highly atmospheric 17th-century fortress that is associated with Champlain, the founder of Quebec. The ramparts are sculpted with Disneyesque watch-towers at the corners, and the citadel, formerly a coastal bastion, is now 3 km (2 miles) from the sea.

The main marshland zone is the regional park of the Marais Poitevin, north of La Rochelle, which is a bit like Venice without the fine buildings. The area used to be the Gulf of Poitou in the 11th century and has been gradually reclaimed since then. Large ditches called 'conches' and channels with densely wooded banks striate the countryside to immensely beautiful effect. Pleasure trips throughout the region may be taken in flat-bottomed punts on the water or by bicycle – or even by horse-drawn caravan – along the banks.

The old port at La Rochelle is celebrated for its non-identical twin towers at the harbour-mouth which had a chain slung between them to make sure ship captains could not slip away without paying their mooring dues. One of the towers was also used as a gaol and you can still see chess boards that the prisoners carved into the wooden floors to help pass the time.

The town still has 15th-century wooden-beamed houses and pretty arcaded streets. There are numerous rather original museums, including themes of the Last War, Automatons and the links between La Rochelle and the Americas. There is a fortified church nearby at Esnandes.

*Splitting the trunk – the pattern of the grain is determined before tapping in a metal wedge at the exact point which will provide a clean split.*

*Louis Victor – artisanal cognac for more than 100 years.*

At the mouth of the Charente lies Rochefort, a military port in the past which now is full of works of art. There are collections from the French, Flemish and Italian schools and Etruscan and Greek ceramics in the Fine Arts museum. The Royal Rope Factory (17th century) is intriguing.

The islands off the coast have assorted attractions. The Ile d'Aix is where Napoleon embarked for St Helena so, of course, there is a Napoleonic museum, but it also has several attractive beaches and 19th-century Fort Boyard, which formerly guarded the Charente estuary, to photograph offshore, or visit if you have a boat. Motor cars are not allowed on the island.

The Ile d'Oléron has a distinctive landscape of low village houses, pine forests and oyster beds by the beaches. Château d'Oléron was a citadel and St Pierre has a 12th-century 'lantern of the dead', an unusual monument that seems closely related to the grave-yard *calvaires* of northern France. There is an appealing little tourist train at St-Trojan and a bird reserve at Les Grissotières. St Georges church is Romanesque.

All around the Ile de Ré are fine sandy beaches with whitewashed villages, vineyards, salt marshes and oyster beds. Sailors used the church spires as landmarks and the mosquito problem used to be so bad that the working donkeys were kitted out with special pantaloons for protection. Rivedoux has an abbey, the pretty port of Ars has a Romanesque portal on the church and there is a lighthouse at Les Baleines. The latter two islands are reached by a toll bridge.

There is a lot to see, from the prehistoric and the classic to the futuristic and the fascinating. Most French towns have their tourist offices (called *syndicats d'initiative*), from which preliminary or on the spot information may be obtained.

## LISTINGS

### Balluet

The Balluet family have grown vines on their own property and made cognac since 1845; they market their artisanal brandies throughout Europe and Britain. M. Balluet makes his cognac from two stills of different sizes. They welcome visitors and if given notice they can probably muster up enough English to show non-French-speakers around.

#### Labels

VSOP; Très Vieille Réserve.

The cognacs that go into these two qualities range from 10 to 40 years in age.

### BALLUET TRÈS VIEILLE RÉSERVE

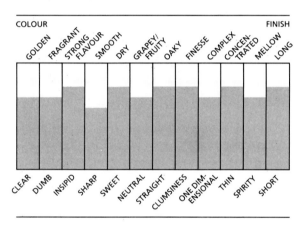

### Bisquit

Alexandre Bisquit was only 20 years-old when he founded his company in Jarnac. Because he was from Limoges he brought oak from there to build his maturing vats, but that same Limousin wood was soon used by all the firms. Bisquit's château at Lignières has the largest vineyard in Cognac and is in the Fins Bois zone.

The storage *chais* are air-conditioned to simulate riverside conditions for ageing the casks and the stillhouse has over 60 stills. Bisquit lets distillation run on to a lower strength than most, helping to render its brandy pleasingly full-flavoured and grapey. It was one of the first firms to sell into China and the Far East and it now exports to over 100 countries.

#### Labels

*** 3yo; VSOP 7yo; Napoléon 22yo; Extra Vieille 50yo; Privilège 100yo.

*M. Bouju has clung to the uncompromised traditions of Grande Champagne in the production of his own cognac.*

### Bouju, Daniel

Bouju is the epitome of a traditional country producer who distils cognac from his own grapes in the top Grande Champagne zone. He is fiercely proud of his uncompromising artisanal methods and the amount of attention he pays to detail. The vintage is hand-picked and he has a 16 hectolitre pot-still as against the more usual 25-hectolitre type.

Back in 1805, an ancestor of M. Bouju called M. Allard started with a tiny 3 hectolitre still. It lasted almost 100 years and was replaced with a 6 hectolitre still in 1900. In 1960 M. Bouju allowed himself the luxury of replacing it in turn with the current 16 hectolitre apparatus. These small stills mean much more successive refilling to obtain a given volume of brouillis or spirit, but they also mean much more control for the distiller. When he knows what he is doing, a greatly superior brandy will result.

Transport in the family's vineyards was horse-hauled up to 1948 when they bought their first tractor. Since the still was wood-fired it had to be watched continuously, which meant that someone had to sleep in the stillroom during distillation runs. Today the family own 20 hectares of Ugni Blanc vines. M. Bouju adds no caramel or sugar, the roundness in his natural cognac stemming from the maturation process.

In the 1970s there was a widespread move towards producing cognac with mass appeal, so M. Bouju began his own marketing in order to retain the uncompromised traditional Grande Champagne characteristics of his own production.

There are nine cognacs in his range and, by his own description, M. Bouju's house-style reminds you of armagnac – 'virile, rustic and substantial', he says – but it is dry and very long in finish. Only length of ageing separates the individual brandies and they are bottled at the time of the sale.

Bouju has excellent cognac stocks which amount to 17 times his annual sales rate, giving him great scope when it comes to making blending decisions.

Exports go throughout Europe, the United States and Japan.

## Labels
**** 4yo (following an old tradition of a star for each year of ageing); VSOP 7yo; Napoléon 10yo; Empereur 15yo; Extra 25yo; Très Vieux 32yo. The following are *brut de fût*, cask-strength according to their different ages: Très Vieux 32yo is 50% abv; Réserve Familiale 50–80yo is 42% abv; Special Cuisine 10yo is 60% abv.

## Bouron, Louis
Cognac Bouron was founded in 1832 and the family distil cognac only from their own vineyards in Petite Champagne, Borderies and Fins Bois. The brandies are aged at the beautiful 13th-century Château de la Grange near Cognac in a 1500-cask store which includes some century-old brandy. The produce of each vineyard is distilled separately and all new spirit goes into new oak. The house-style is light, dry, smooth and aromatic. The company have another label, Maxim's de Paris, (q.v.) by arrangement with the famous restaurant.

## Labels
*** 5yo; Prestige 6yo; VSOP 8yo; Blason d'Or 12yo; Napoléon 18–20yo; Grande Réserve 25yo; Très Vieille Réserve 35yo; XO 30yo.

### BOURON BLASON D'OR

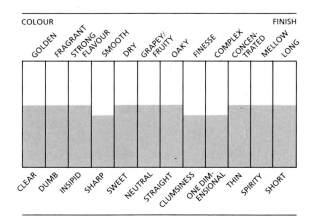

### BOURON GRANDE RÉSERVE

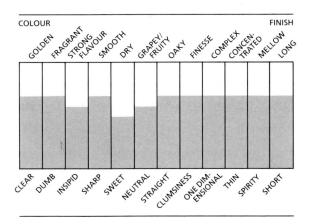

*Louis Bouron distils only from his own vineyards – the produce of each vineyard is distilled separately.*

## BOURON TRÈS VIEILLE RÉSERVE

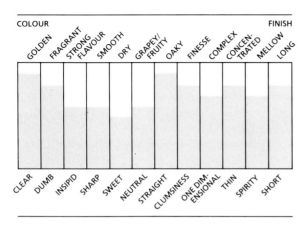

## BOURON XO

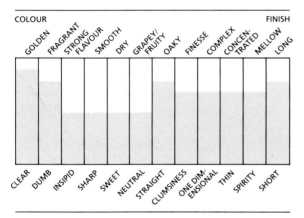

### Camus

Camus was founded in 1863 and was perhaps the first to use a brand name, 'La Grande Marque'. Jean-Baptiste Camus was a smallholder who broke loose from the dominance of the big buyers and formed a consortium with other landowners.

Today the firm is based in Cognac and has vineyards and châteaux in the Grande Champagne and Borderies zones. Each of the four châteaux has its own distillery but Camus also buys in old cognacs, usually between 20 and 50 years of age, for blending. It built up export business in Russia and today it tops the world sales league in premium cognacs. It also produces almost a quarter of it.

Camus' most successful brand is the Napoléon, which makes up 60% of their turnover and which forms a fifth of all cognac sold in this category. The firm has a strong presence in duty-free shops worldwide.

*Camus tops the world sales league in premium cognacs, and at one time was an accredited supplier to the Czar of Russia.*

### Labels

**\*\*\*** Célébration; VSOP Grand; Napoléon; Extra; XO: Napoléon Vieille Réserve.

## CAMUS XO

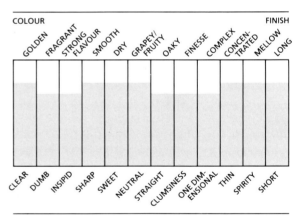

### Courvoisier

A former world brand-leader and still one of the top three firms, Courvoisier has been based in Jarnac since 1790, early enough to gain its prime office site on the town's main square. Its connection with Napoléon stems from an account of British naval officers sampling his supply of Courvoisier on board ship and later referring appreciatively to Napoléon's cognac; 'le cognac de

Napoléon' became the slogan used by the firm. The company was later made accredited supplier to Napoléon III.

Owned by an English family from 1909 to 1963, the firm successfully re-emerged in the post-war period after confiscation by the Germans. Courvoisier owns no vineyards or distilleries, buying instead from several hundred producers, many of whom have supplied young cognacs to it for generations in the style it likes. The firm then ages and blends them in its own cellars. The general style is quite full, round and rich. Courvoisier exports to 160 countries.

Visitors are welcome to the museum from May to October inclusive. It has Napoléonic memorabilia – including the famous hat – and explains the details of cognac-production.

### Labels
VS; VSOP Fine Champagne; Napoléon Fine Champagne; XO; Initiale Extra; also a range of special editions, including a decanter painted by the artist Erté.

## COURVOISIER XO

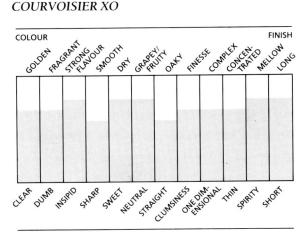

## Delamain
This is a highly exclusive family firm which deals only in old cognacs from top zone Grande Champagne. It holds no vineyards of its own, but buys, ages and blends old brandies for its four prestigious brands, the 'youngest' of which has a 25-year average age.

Delamain has been associated with cognac-production since 1759, but an earlier member of the family went to England in 1625 as part of the court of King Charles I, and subsequently moved on to Ireland where he established an important porcelain factory.

The present chairman's father formerly ran Courvoisier (q.v.) and family members have distinguished themselves in a wide range of fields such as archaeology, entomology, publishing and writing. In 1937 Robert Delamain wrote a definitive book on cognac which is still in print today.

Slow, gentle ageing in well-used oak is a Delamain feature, making its cognacs pale and dry – hence the well-known brand-name. The brandies are exported all over the world, but production is small – 50,000 cases.

### Labels
Pale & Dry 25yo; Vesper 35yo; Très Vénérable 85yo; Réserve de la Famille 60yo is unblended, natural strength of 42% abv.

## DELAMAIN PALE & DRY

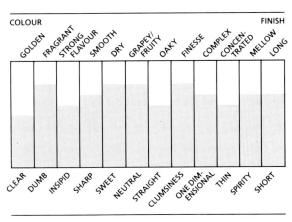

## DELAMAIN TRÈS VÉNÉRABLE

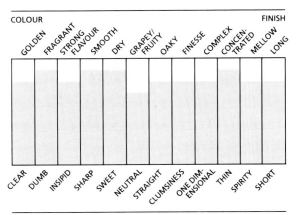

## DELAMAIN RÉSERVE DE LA FAMILLE

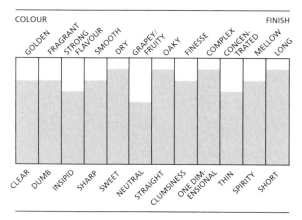

## DENIS-MOUNIÉ EXTRA

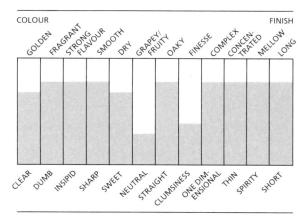

### Denis-Mounié

Justin Denis and Henri Mounié set up in business together in 1838 to produce the best cognac they possibly could. That they succeeded seems to be borne out by the company's becoming, in 1908, the first cognac house to receive the warrant to supply the British royal family. King Edward VII granted this honour and the company reciprocated by naming its 20-year-old Fine Champagne after him. King George V continued the warrant, and Denis-Mounié is the only cognac firm to have been twice warrant-holders in the UK.

The company buys spirit and ages it in its own cellars. It exports mainly throughout Europe and to the Far East, with Japan particularly important. There are no visitor facilities.

### Labels
*** 4yo; VSOP 8yo; Edouard VII 20yo; Extra 30yo.

## DENIS-MOUNIÉ EDOUARD VII

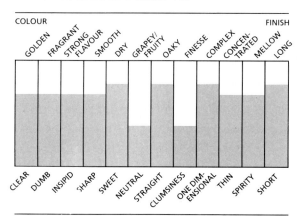

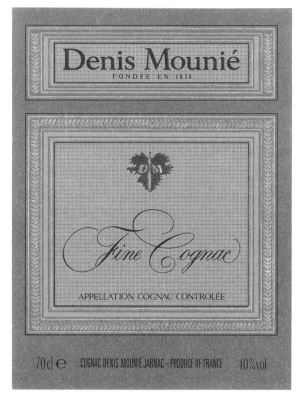

*Denis Mounié was the first cognac house to receive the warrant to supply the British royal family.*

### Exshaw

No 1 and Age d'Or are both de luxe Grande Champagne cognacs. No 1 is officially a ten-year-old but there is 40-year-old spirit in the blend. Age d'Or's mix contains some 100-year-old brandy and is available in a globular decanter as well as in the standard bottle swathed in a yellow bag with the Napoleonic coat of arms stamped on it. A rather over-the-top promotional taste profile describes Exshaw cognac as more Botticelli than Rubens.

The Lord Mayor of Dublin in 1770 was a John Exshaw and a descendant of the same name made his way to Bordeaux in 1802, where he joined Huguenot uncles in business. He began ageing cognac there and exported it to the Far East, having his ships fly American flags to enable them to beat the British blockade of France. He was the first to export bottled cognac via Suez, but he did it before the canal had been built – the cases were carried across the isthmus by camel.

Thomas-Henri, son of John, did much of the trail-blazing for cognac around the world by travelling throughout the then enormous and far-flung British Empire. You could stumble out of the Malayan jungle or surface in a Chinese entrepôt and find Exshaw cognac on the sideboard or bar shelf. Britain's loss of the Empire meant Exshaw's loss of many of the more outlandish markets, and it led the company to pioneer the now-widespread policy of concentrating on expensive top-end qualities.

## EXSHAW NO. 1

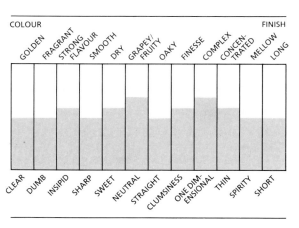

## EXSHAW AGE D'OR

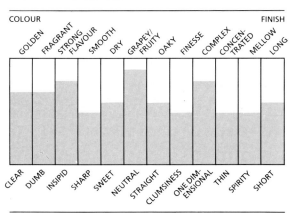

### Ferrand, Pierre

An award-winning craftsman-made cognac from Grande Champagne by a distiller who believes that the brandy should not be sold before it has aged for 15 years. It takes 12 years in cask before it 'turns', says M. Ferrand, and the young alcohol and ethers are finally lost. He does none of the usual commercial grades like VSOP, Napoléon etc., preferring to sell 'very old' cognacs with given names.

The Ferrand family are 12th-generation owners of the vineyards from which all their cognac is made. Distillation methods are utterly traditional, essentially as they were when the estate was formed in 1702. There are two stills and distillation is carried out in small 1500 litre (330 gal) batches. M. Ferrand adds nothing – no caramel, sugar or boisé – to his brandies, which are produced entirely on the property, from growing the grapes to bottling the finished cognac.

Exports are greatly in demand in the United States, Japan and Europe at very high prices. Ferrand have another brand, also Grande Champagne, called Pierre Joseph (q.v.). Visitors are welcome and, if you speak French, M. Ferrand himself will show you around.

### Labels

Réserve de la Propieté 15–25yo in bottle or crystal decanter; Sélection des Anges 25–35yo in bottle or Sèvres crystal decanter; Réserve Ancestrale in a hand-blown bottle is from family stocks that date from the turn of the century. Only 200 bottles are released each year. The most recent bottling is from a 1924 distillate.

## FERRAND RÉSERVE DE LA PROPRIÉTÉ

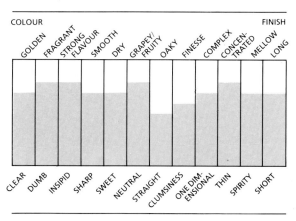

## FERRAND SÉLECTION DES ANGES

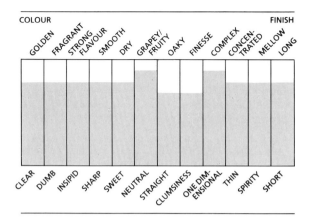

## VIEILLE RÉSERVE FINE CHAMPAGNE

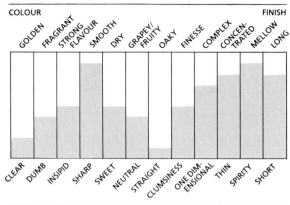

### Fussigny, A. de

Alain Royer disagreed with the production policy of the Louis Royer firm run by his father, so he left to set up de Fussigny with his wife (whose maiden name this is). He blends a range of old cognacs that are elegant and svelte with a fresh persona and modern watercolour bottle labels. Three years into the business de Fussigny sells around 2000 cases a year of top-end brandy. The lot numbers will change as each assemblage, or blend, is exhausted and new batches are created.

Eighty per cent of production is exported to the United States, Japan and the rest of Europe.

### Labels

XO Lot 099 15–40yo is from the Champagnes and Fins Bois; Heritage Lot 102 is 70% Petite Champagne; Fine Champagne Vieille Réserve 20/30yo has 60% Grande Champagne; Très Vieille Grande Champagne 50yo is from 1937 distillate. The hand-blown bottles are reproductions of 19th-century Bordeaux bottles.

## DE FUSSIGNY XO LOT 099

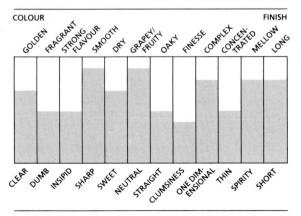

## TRÈS VIEILLE GRANDE CHAMPAGNE

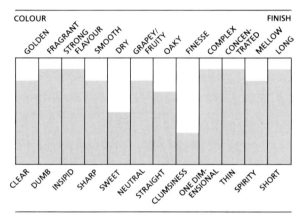

### Gautier

In 1644 Charles Gautier bought vineyards and settled in Aigre, which lay on the 'Royal Route' between Paris and Bordeaux. This regal 'passing trade' made the town important so it was here, in the midst of what became the Fins Bois vineyard zone, that his grandson Louis set up in the cognac business in 1755.

Aigre is not generally thought of as a cognac town today, but at the beginning of the 19th century there were almost as many cognac firms in Aigre as there were in Cognac itself. Over the decades, Gautier cognac has cropped up in most of the main high-life locations, including the famous cruise ships in their heyday, and it was served at the investiture of the Prince of Wales in 1911.

No-one could say that the Gautier casks lack their quota of damp country air in which to mature; the ageing cellars are located on the site of an old watermill on a little island in a tributary river of the Charente itself.

Gautier cognacs win competition awards, and the XO decanter is elegant, but they also shine in the field of kitsch packaging.

There is a remarkable porcelain decanter in the form of the Concorde jet aeroplane (the French version, of course) that comes in purple or white and gold; a fishing-net float suspended in a twine hammock inside a ship's wheel; and another float done up as a ship's lantern with a rope handle (containing XO cognac, no less).

### Labels

VS; VSOP; Napoléon; XO; Royale; Extra Crystal in an elegant, long-necked decanter.

### Gautret, Jules

This is the export label used mainly in Europe by the large cooperative Unicognac (q.v.), based in Jonzac.

### Labels

***; VSOP Fine Champagne; Napoléon.

### Godet

The Godet family are of Dutch origin and their forbears settled in the Charente region around 1600. Henri IV used to buy Godet's 'burnt wine' and eventually granted the family the right to wear swords, a signal honour at the time. They exported to England during the whole of the 17th century and then, in 1838, they moved to La Rochelle and began developing sales in bottle under their own name.

Godet is a firm that unusually combines the production of good cognac with a somewhat kitsch range of novelty bottles, notably Limoges porcelain anchors and a bust of Napoleon. An innovation is a narrow bottle specially made to fit into an attaché case. The United States is the company's main export market but its cognacs reach 47 countries around the world.

### Labels

***; VSOP; VSOP Gastronome Fine Champagne 10 yo uses a blend created by Gédéon Godet in 1840; Extra Vieille Réserve Grande Champagne. In addition a collection of specials: Excellence 25yo is from the Champagnes and Borderies; XO 30yo is Fine Champagne sold in an old-style Italian decanter; Renaissance 50yo is Grande Champagne in a crystal decanter; St Louis is another 50-year-old, this time Fine Champagne in a crystal decanter.

## GODET GASTRONOME

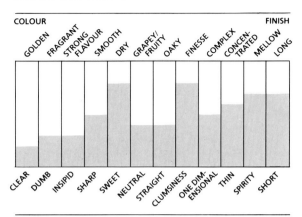

## GODET EXCELLENCE FINE CHAMPAGNE

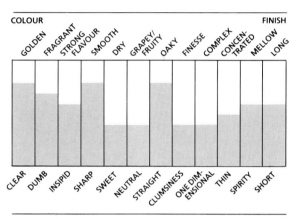

## GODET XO

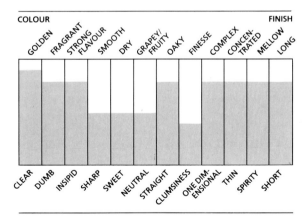

## Hennessy

'Hennessy' was said to be the only 'gringo' word the notorious Pancho Villa liked to hear. Richard Hennessy was a captain in the Irish Brigade of Louis XIV's army and, duty over, he stayed in France. He founded the company in Cognac in 1765 and today it is the world-leader.

Everything is on a grand scale – the firm has 2500 contracted vine-growers, 28 distilleries, the largest stocks of maturing cognac (200 000 casks of it) and it even has its own forest of Limousin oak. About 98% of its production is exported and annual sales reach 33 million bottles. The United States is Hennessy's biggest market, with Japan and Britain next in line.

Six generations of the Fillioux family have been its head-tasters; the tasting team use a detailed technical glossary that enables them to make 200 precise assessments of spirits. It was a Hennessy who first used stars to designate a cognac's worth, as well as the term XO. This is another firm that likes to produce full, fruity and rich cognac. The company also owns the best-selling grape brandy brand 'Three Barrels' (q.v.) through its Raynal subsidiary.

Visitors are welcome; indeed, over 75,000 visitors call every year and there are cognac and cooperage museums to take in.

### Labels

VS 2½yo is Hennessy's biggest-selling type, a blend of four zones; VSOP 4yo is Fine Champagne; Napoléon 7yo; XO 10yo; Paradis 15yo, which always has a smidgin of 100yo in it, sells in a decanter.

### HENNESSY NAPOLÉON

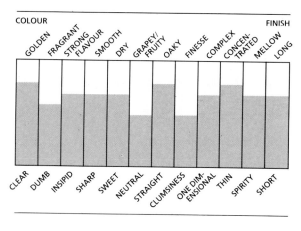

## Hine

Thomas Hine went to France in 1792 from Dorset in England and was stranded there by the French Revolution. He got work in Jarnac, married the boss's daughter and showed such flair for the family cognac business that he took it over and changed its name to his own.

Today, the Hine cousins Jacques and Bernard buy in cognacs to age and blend them in small casks to a delicate and svelte house-style, and Hine is the only cognac firm at present holding a warrant to supply the British royal family. Early-landed vintage cognacs are something of a speciality, the 15-year minimum ages attained in the damp of English bonded warehouses guarded by the British Customs.

Signature is not designated *** because it is widely regarded as better than many of the VSOPs around. It derives from both Champagnes and the Fins Bois zones. All new spirits spend the first eight months in new wood and then go into tronçais casks seasoned with cognac. No boisé whatsoever is added. Over 45 years of age, the cognacs are carefully monitored to decide when they should be transferred to glass demijohns to avoid their becoming too woody. Bottles are rinsed with cognac before being filled and reference samples of each release are kept for ten years.

Hine exports throughout Europe, to the United States and to the Far East.

### Labels

Signature; VSOP (Fine Champagne) 8–10yo; Antique (Fine Champagne), 20–25yo; Triomphe (Grande Champagne) 45yo; Family Réserve (Grande Champagne) 60–70yo; various Early-landed Late-bottled.

### HINE ANTIQUE

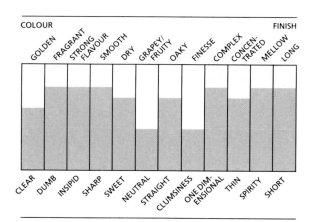

# HINE TRIOMPHE

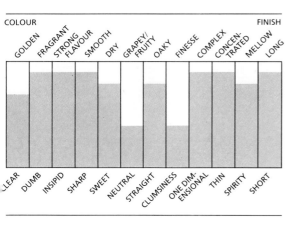

| COLOUR | | | | | | | | | | | | FINISH |
| GOLDEN | FRAGRANT | STRONG FLAVOUR | SMOOTH | DRY | GRAPEY/FRUITY | OAKY | FINESSE | COMPLEX | CONCEN-TRATED | MELLOW | LONG |
|--------|----------|----------------|--------|-----|---------------|------|---------|---------|---------------|--------|------|
| CLEAR | DUMB | INSIPID | SHARP | SWEET | NEUTRAL | STRAIGHT | CLUMSINESS | ONE DIM-ENSIONAL | THIN | SPIRITY | SHORT |

# HINE FAMILY RESERVE

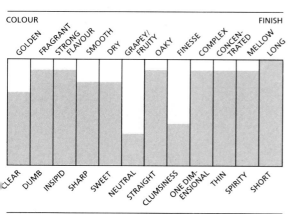

| COLOUR | | | | | | | | | | | | FINISH |
| GOLDEN | FRAGRANT | STRONG FLAVOUR | SMOOTH | DRY | GRAPEY/FRUITY | OAKY | FINESSE | COMPLEX | CONCEN-TRATED | MELLOW | LONG |
|--------|----------|----------------|--------|-----|---------------|------|---------|---------|---------------|--------|------|
| CLEAR | DUMB | INSIPID | SHARP | SWEET | NEUTRAL | STRAIGHT | CLUMSINESS | ONE DIM-ENSIONAL | THIN | SPIRITY | SHORT |

*Hine cognacs are blended and aged in small casks from 15 to 45 years.*

### Joseph, Pierre
These are very fine, complex cognacs which are hand-made with great care and expertise on the estate of Pierre Ferrand (q.v.).

### Labels
Réserve Famille 15yo, in bottle or decanter; Age d'Or 25yo in bottle or decanter; L'Ancêtre is from spirit distilled in 1923.

### Lafite
This is the Lafite that produces the celebrated Rothschild Premier Cru claret at Pauillac near Bordeaux.

It was launched just a few years ago with the help of Alain Royer, of the Louis Royer family (q.v.), who has subsequently gone into business separately as de Fussigny (q.v.).

### Label
Très Vieille Réserve, a high-quality, polished old cognac with rounded intensity and a long, smoky finish.

### Lanxner, R & B
Not the most famous of the company names that deal in cognac, but it has one very important distinction – this is a Kosher cognac. Nothing is left out, nothing extra is put in. It tastes as good cognac should do, but its production is supervised to ensure that nothing goes against the precepts that would deny it rabbinical approval.

### Labels
***; VSOP; Napoléon.

### Martell
Jean Martell travelled from the Island of Jersey to Cognac in 1715 and settled there. He established his business on a prime site in the centre of town and the company, now gigantic, is still there today. Martell is involved in most aspects of the cognac business, partly because it has to, due to its volume of business.

The firm has extensive vineyard holdings in the top four production zones, but it also buys wines and distillates from about 2800 growers and distillers in those same locations. And, of course, it ages and blends. The house-style has an earthy, nutty signature that comes from careful use of Borderies spirit to give the lead characteristic. Like Hennessy, Martell has had many consecutive generations of the one family – the Chapeau – as its head blenders/tasters. It exports to every market where cognac is drunk.

Visitors are welcome all through the year, but telephone for opening times.

### Labels
VS 5yo; Médaillon VSOP 10yo; Cordon Rubis 15yo; Cordon Noir Napoléon 18yo; Cordon Bleu 24yo; Cordon Argent Extra 55yo.

## MARTELL CORDON BLEU

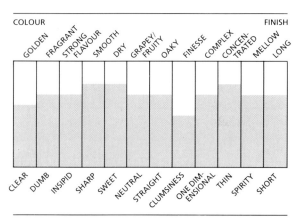

*The Maxim's de Paris range of upmarket cognacs is produced by Cognac Buron.*

## Maxim's de Paris
A limited range of upmarket cognacs produced by arrangement with the well-known restaurant by S. A. Château de la Grange, who market Cognac Bouron (q.v.).

The *fin de siècle* presentation of the bottles is very attractive and incorporates the distinctive Maxim visuals on the labels.

### Labels
VSOP 8–10yo; Napoléon 20yo; XO 30yo.

## MAXIM'S DE PARIS VSOP

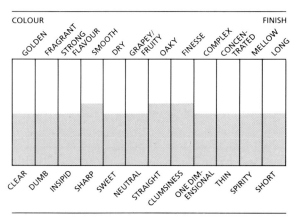

## MAXIM'S NAPOLÉON

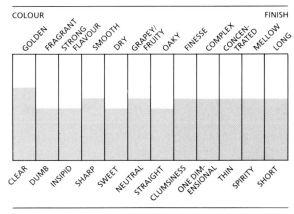

## MAXIM'S XO

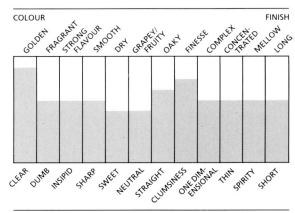

## Otard

The ancestral line of the founder of Otard includes a Viking noble, a soldier who fought at the side of William the Conqueror in the Battle of Hastings in 1066 and a Scottish baron. The ruins of Dunottar Castle on the Scottish coast near Aberdeen were the romantic backdrop for an Otard family wedding recently.

Jean Otard was sentenced to death in the French Revolution but escaped. When he returned home he used family stocks of old cognac to set up in business with a partner, distilling and blending brandies. Within a year he bought the Château de Cognac on the bank of the Charente river to furnish more storage space; it dates from the ninth century and was the birthplace of King François I of France. The firm's cognacs still mature there.

By 1800 Otard was so important that he bought the entire Cognac grape crop in that year. The company always dealt in casks-sales and refused to join the bottle trade, averring 'We are not grocers.' This caused problems and in the 1930s the family's majority shareholding was sold.

The distinctive Otard bottle-shape comes from the teardrop shape of the brandy that 'weeps' down the inside of the glass after it has been swirled. The XO sells in a similarly shaped crystal decanter version, and the Extra in porcelain.

Visitors are welcome.

### Labels
*** 3yo blend of Borderies, Fins Bois and Bons Bois; VSOP 8yo Fine Champagne; Napoléon 15yo in bottle or crystal decanter; XO 35yo mainly Champagne blends; Extra 50yo mainly Champagne blends. The latter two are matured in 'russet' – very gentle – old casks and show the rancio flavour of very old brandies.

### OTARD XO

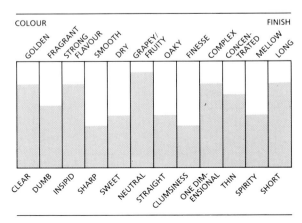

### OTARD EXTRA

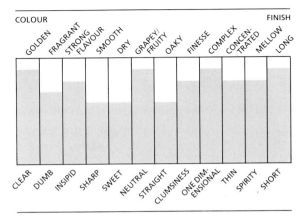

## Polignac

This is the main brand of the Unicoop co-operative which was created in 1929 to produce, store, age and market the members' cognac. There are 3500 affiliated growers, 15% of them from the Champagnes. Sixty pot-stills distil 30 million litres of wine each year and the cellars have a capacity of 28 000 casks. Polignac has the Paul Bocuse brand, named for the great chef, and blended as Fine Champagne.

The Polignac family goes back to the ninth century and settled for a while in the Auvergne where they built a splendid fortress on a rock. Polignacs have been cardinals, ministers and soldiers over the centuries and the Duchess Yolande was one of the most honoured aides to Louis XIV and Marie Antoinette. The Prince gave permission in 1947 for Unicoop to use his name for this brand.

The United States is the brand's best export market, worth 2.5 million cases, followed by Japan and the United Kingdom.

Visitors are welcome; telephone for details.

### Labels
***; VSOP 4–20yo; Napoléon 6–30yo; XO 10–50yo; Dynastie Hors d'Age Grande Champagne. Also special editions in Limoges porcelain flask decanters and Sèvres crystal decanters; and assorted novelty packagings.

## Prunier

Prunier is small compared to the giants who jostle the market place. It does have a staple range but its forte is the top-end of cognac quality, where it not only has splendid brandies but is also resourceful. Vintage cognacs have been forbidden in recent years because proof has been so difficult to show, so 20 years ago Prunier began lodging casks in French state bonded warehouses. It is now able to market a 20-year-old vintage cognac since it has state documentation as proof. The current vintage is 1967. The older qualities are orientated towards the United States market and the house-style shows good fruit-and-nut core within gentle smoothness.

Jean Prunier began exporting cognac as early as 1700 from La Rochelle, and in the early 1800s the family moved to Cognac. During the 19th century Prunier cognac was drunk around the world, even in Australia, where Gaston Prunier had set up a company branch. The old house shown as the Prunier trademark is the medieval Maison de la Lieutenance in Cognac which is now owned by Prunier and may be seen by visitors.

### Labels
***; VSOP; Napoléon; Family Réserve Grande Champagne; Château de Brives, a 15-year-old single-property cognac from Prunier's own vineyard in the Petite Champagne zone; Vintage 20 year-old; XO 15–40yo Grande Champagne.

## PRUNIER FAMILY RESERVE

## PRUNIER CHÂTEAU DE BRIVES

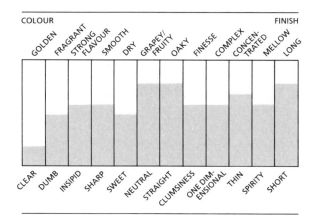

## PRUNIER 20 YEAR-OLD

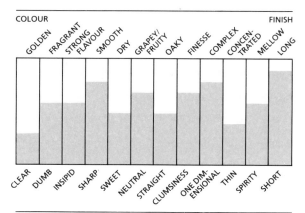

## PRUNIER XO

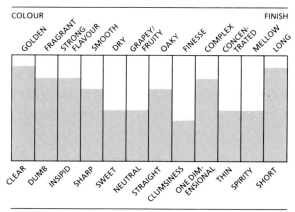

### Rémy Martin
The company was set up in 1724 by a grower in Grande Champagne, so it is appropriate that Rémy Martin's spectacular success as the world's top VSOP should derive from its specializing in cognac

exclusively from the Champagne zones. It was the first to make a feature of VSOP from Fine Champagne – Grande (minimum 50%) and Petite Champagne blended – and today that approach helps it sell more VSOP than all the other VSOPs put together.

Despite the volume attained, the youngest cognac in the blend is seven-years-old. The requirement for brandies from these two top zones is such that only one of the firm's range is exclusively Grande Champagne – the very top Rémy Martin brand, Louis XIII. It is a blend of very old cognacs, the youngest of which is over 50 years. The decanter is a replica of one found on the site of the Battle of Jarnac in 1569.

The house style is middle-of-the-road with the younger brands but blossoms with good vanilla mellowness in the older blends, the result of careful wood-management using smaller than usual casks. At the Grande Champagne village of Merpins, Remy have the equivalent of 160 million bottles in stocks of cognac – eight years' sales at their turnover rate, and the largest reserves of Fine Champagne in the world.

Séguin-Moreau is perhaps the world's best-known cooperage, and it is Europe's biggest. Rémy own it and – logically – it is near those mighty brandy stocks at Merpins.

About 96% of the company's sales are exports and they reach 165 different countries.

## Labels
***; VSOP; Club; Napoléon; XO Special; Extra. Also Excellence and Centaure, sold in Limoges porcelain. All of these are Fine Champagne. Louis XIII from Grande Champagne is the oldest in the range, sold in a Baccarat crystal decanter.

### REMY MARTIN VSOP

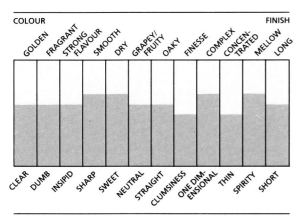

## Renault
The firm was established in 1835, the very year that it is thought cognac was first sold in bottles, and Renault was one of the first companies to adopt the new idea. It merged with the Castillon company which had been founded in 1814 and whose name was still used as a cognac brand until about ten years ago.

Renault is a distiller, buying in wine from growers in the four main vineyard zones. Carte Noire is described as 'Napoléon-type' and is aimed in price terms between VSOP and Napoléon to attract consumers in both categories. The strongest markets for the firm are northern Europe and world-wide duty-frees, selling about 130 000 cases a year.

### Label
Carte Noire Extra 20yo.

### RENAULT CARTE NOIR EXTRA

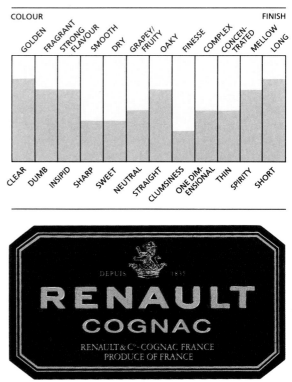

## Roi des Rois
One of the brands of the Unicognac co-operative founded in 1847 at Jonzac in the Petite Champagne. By an extraordinary coincidence, Unicognac and rival co-operative Unicoop declare the same number of members and the same vineyard area owned – 3500 and 5000 hectares (12 354

acres) respectively. There are 16 pot-stills in the modern Unicognac distillery at Mosnac and the co-operative sells about two million bottles annually, mostly to North America, Europe and Japan. Its other brands are Ansac, which is the eighth-ranking cognac in the United States, and Jules Gautret in Europe.

This is another operation with a notable line in kitsch decanters, including a gold paint-flecked white porcelain rendering of Napoléon on a rearing horse which looks more like the Lone Ranger caught in a blizzard. For those curious to know how the wine of Cognac tastes, Unicoop produce a modest but authentic wine from Ugni Blanc and Colombard grapes grown on nine of the co-operative estates.

### Labels
VS; VSOP; XO Fine Champagne; Extra Hors d'Age Grande Champagne.

### ROIS DES ROIS XO

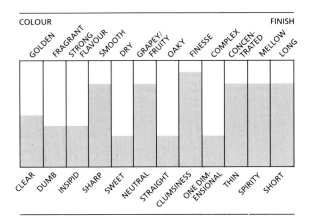

### ROI DES ROIS EXTRA HORS D'AGE

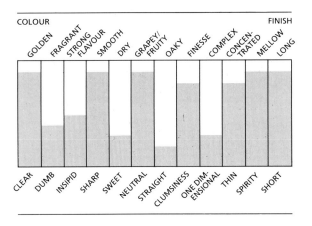

### Royer, Louis

A well-established firm which has a Fine Champagne range of the usual types but which has tended mainly to supply volume brandy. This was the basis of the family split when a son, Alain, wanted to do more at the high-quality end of the business; he left to set up a new label, de Fussigny (q.v.), with his wife. Louis Royer now belongs to the Japanese giant Suntory.

### Victor, Louis

A small company at Saint-Maigrin that has been producing artisanal cognac for more than a century. Its style is light, soft and not too dry. The brandies it uses in its blends range from five to 40 years of age and it produces 10 000 bottles a year. A quarter of its production goes to Germany and a little goes to Holland, but most sells within France. Visits are possible by prior arrangement.

### Labels
*** 5yo; VSOP; Vieux Cognac.

### LOUIS VICTOR

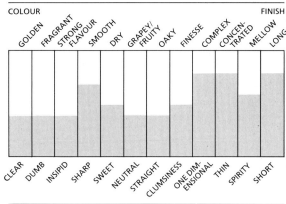

*Louis Victor – light and soft artisanal cognacs.*

# GRAPE BRANDY – ARMAGNAC

Armagnac, the brandy of D'Artagnan and the Three Musketeers, is the other main appellation contrôlée grape brandy of France. Many believe it to be just as important as cognac, albeit not as famous. Like cognac, armagnac takes its name from the region where it is produced and, although comparisons are inevitably made between the two, it is very much a product in its own right, displaying its own distinctive attributes.

Its flavour is fuller and rounder than that of cognac and it is more aromatic; the traditional distillation method is different, as is the soil in which the grapes grow; and the region's people, the Armagnacais, were making their brandy well before the Cognaçais began producing theirs.

Unlike cognac, armagnac is available in single vintages, some of them going back to the last century. Single-property armagnacs are more easily tracked down than cognacs.

*In Armagnac, plums, prunes and raspberries are the most universal flavour notes picked up by the sampler, while general flower presence typifies the bouquet in the glass.*

For the brandy amateur who enjoys seeking out individuality from small producers, armagnac offers almost unlimited scope. This is because, while the generic identity is firmly fixed by the regulations specifying the type of grapes that may be used, there is considerable variation in the regional and 'house' styles of the brandy itself, rather as in the single malt whiskies of Scotland or the classed growth clarets of Bordeaux.

This is further expanded by the fact that the cognac pot-still, which produces a finer, less assertive spirit, may now be legally used to make armagnac in addition to the continuous still, so there are two distinct styles of product – which may also be blended to span the complete scale between the two types.

Worldwide, armagnac sells only about 6% of the number of bottles of cognac sold each year but, although the number of bottles sold has not dramatically increased in recent years, the value certainly has. People are recognizing the prestige and quality of armagnac and are buying at the expensive old-vintage and single-property end of the range.

It is not so much the French themselves who are doing this – they mainly buy young armagnac for mixing at the cheaper end of the scale – as seekers of distinguished bottles in Japan, the UK and the USA.

Good armagnac is not cheaper than cognac but it can offer greater scope for choice and cachet.

### The countryside
Geographically, Armagnac is part of the ancient region of Gascony in south-west France, the substantial chunk of countryside south of Bordeaux which tourists heading for the Pyrenees usually underestimate and which thus completely throws out their travel schedules.

It is a peaceful, rural and green landscape, combining woodland, orchards, fields of sunflowers, maize and grass, castles, vineyards and sleepy villages. The railway never crossed it so it has remained relatively undeveloped, with its most famous industries – pâté de foie gras and armagnac brandy – still largely artisanal affairs rooted in the farmhouses and *basses-cours* that are sewn into the landscape.

### History
Wood-working Gauls in the Armagnac area developed the cask which came to be used for making and storing beer, wine and eau-de-vie.

*The wine which is produced from the folle blanche grape, although bitingly acidic, will distil into a fine aromatic brandy.*

Armagnac is very likely France's oldest brandy, the region's inhabitants having learned about distillation by the 12th century through contacts with the Moors on the other side of the Pyrenees on the Iberian peninsula.

Certainly, by 1411 there was documentation that distillation was being carried out in the region, and throughout the Middle Ages armagnac distillers traded with the Dutch and the British, albeit with some difficulty. Because the region is inland, the producers of armagnac lacked the easy, continuous contact with traders from the north enjoyed by the merchants and distillers of Cognac and Bordeaux.

Ready access to commerce was certainly practicable downriver at Bordeaux, but the Bordelais kept the Gascons out in order to protect their own trade in wines and eaux-de-vie. The Gascons circumvented the ban by selling out of the port of Bayonne, but Armagnac's inland location is one of the reasons that armagnac never became a standardized 'golden mean' product like cognac. Nevertheless, there was good demand for armagnac from the Dutch, and eventually it acquired a settled reputation of sorts.

Up to the beginning of the 19th century the pot-still as used for making cognac was employed, but after some experimentation a local man called Verdier invented a new method of continuous distillation which quickly found favour with armagnac-makers. This new '*alambic armagnacais*' first appeared in 1850, and it was also around this time that many of today's well-known production companies were formed.

The wine-growing zones were delimited in 1909 and in 1936 the Verdier still was made compulsory, although in 1972 pot-stills were once again permitted in addition to the traditional style.

Wider distribution around the world has been made possible in recent years through the whole or partial acquisition of a number of leading armagnac firms by some of the large cognac companies, like Martell and Camus, and other drinks mammoths such as Pernod.

This has meant active advertising and promotion of some brands, something that was rarely possible in the past.

### The brandy

The flavour of armagnac is more fully-stated than that of cognac, with great depth of grapey fruit, richness and intensity of aroma. This is not the caramel-induced roundness found in more modest brandies elsewhere, but the result of its traditional distillation process which produces spirit at a comparatively low still strength which thus carries over more congeners – the esters and flavour-elements from the soil – into the final distillate.

Armagnac's great intensity does not mean it cannot be elegant and complex. Plums, prunes and raspberries are the most universal flavour notes picked up by samplers, while violets and general floral presence seem to typify the bouquet in the glass.

### Single vintage and declared age

There is a remarkable range of vintage armagnac still available, the happy result of the brandy's being almost unknown outside France. Nor is it a matter of having to trace just one or two firms; quite a large number of them have ranges that go back as far as the 1880s, and they are apparently genuine. Carbon 14 dating techniques, usually used in archaeology, can also verify the age of a brandy.

Small parcels of these precious brandies are exported more widely than one might expect, considering their lack of celebrity, so you do not always have to go to France to browse. The USA, Japan, Switzerland and West Germany take regular shipments and interest is growing. Some vintaged brandies from single estates are also to be found.

Single-vintage armagnacs are not necessarily outstanding since harvests, producers and storage conditions can vary enormously, but when you do come across one there is always an excellent chance that it will be fine, aromatic and mellow.

Declared-age brandies – 20 years old, 30 years old etc – are a better bet if you must forswear adventure and seek guarantees. They are usually balanced blends of mature spirits, assembled to dovetail perfectly with each other, the youngest of which will be of the age printed on the label.

The old blends of the main proprietary brands which use the conventional label terms like XO, Napoléon, are utterly reliable, and an important feature of armagnac is that small-production vintages and declared ages have individuality, are eminently explorable and usually extremely rewarding.

## Single-estate armagnacs

Although it is a fact that the most delectable and cornerless armagnacs are likely to be blends, many enthusiasts may prefer the style of a particular zone, or a specific producer, or simply a bit more individuality. This is where single-estate brandies give such wide scope for originality or emphasis while remaining generically correct.

These are the ultimate in hand-crafted, fine-tuned armagnacs: what you get is exactly what the distiller wants you to taste from the bottle with his name on it. Some of these domaine brandies are even matured in casks made from oaks that are grown on the producer's own estate. In addition, domaine brandies will often also be taken from a single vintage.

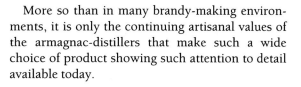

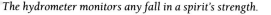
*The hydrometer monitors any fall in a spirit's strength.*

More so than in many brandy-making environments, it is only the continuing artisanal values of the armagnac-distillers that make such a wide choice of product showing such attention to detail available today.

## Vineyard zones

There are three delimited grape-growing zones in the Armagnac region. Bas (Lower) Armagnac has mainly clay soil which yields the best spirits; they have fruit and suppleness. Ténarèze has a mix of clay and chalk soils which gives more powerful brandy with long-lasting, violet-scented aromas. Haut (Upper) Armagnac produces a spirit which in general is less good, showing coarseness and poorer balance. A few good brandies originate from here but most are used in fruit-preserving.

Each of these geographical names may be used on labels where appropriate, but if a blend contains brandy from more than one zone it must be described simply as armagnac.

## Grapes

The main grape variety is the Ugni Blanc but traditionally the Folle Blanche was grown as in Cognac until problems with grafting and susceptibility to disease made it unreliable in the vineyard. Its local name is the Picquepoul, old dialect for *pique-lèvres* (lip-stinger), which is appropriate in view of the bitingly acidic wine it produces but which, as is also the case with cognac, distils so well into fine brandy. A tiny amount is still stubbornly grown, but Ugni Blanc supplies the main volume of wine and there are 10 other eligible vines.

## Distillation

The traditional alambic armagnacais is made of copper and is a type of continuous still developed by Verdier after a succession of experiments by three different men during the first half of the 19th century.

The alambic distils continuously as long as wine is fed into it, and it has the merits of being cheaper to operate and less labour-intensive than a pot-still. In distillation terms it is highly inefficient – a Coffey continuous still can produce to alcoholic strength of 96% while the Verdier delivers spirit at 52–55% abv – but it is precisely this rustic limitation which refines the spirit less, allows more of the richness and flavour from the soil to be carried over in the distillate and endows armagnac with its particularity.

*For many locals, tasting the new armagnac is one of the high points of the year.*

Previously, the cognac pot-still was used and, after a period of proscription, it was readmitted as an alternative means of distillation for armagnac. It requires double distillation and fresh recharging with separate batches of wine after each run, but the firms using them are prepared to cope with the extra work and costs because the stronger, lighter and purer spirit yielded gives greater blending and stylistic flexibility.

Its use arouses passionate debate, however, and it has confused the issue of armagnac's identity. Its worth is still being assessed, although it seems well-suited to the production of high-volume, young brandy – something that has become necessary to restore depleted stocks after years of underpricing armagnac in order to try to gain a market share.

Verdier stills outnumber pot-stills by about three to one throughout the region and there is a handful left of the charming mobile stills which, during the late autumn and winter, trundle around the countryside from site to site like little old Heath Robinson locomotives.

## Maturation

Armagnac is traditionally aged in the black oak of the local Monlezun forest, a wood that imparts generous flavour and bouquet elements to the spirit and a faster maturation rate than lighter oaks give. It is dried out of doors for five years, one year for each centimetre of the thickness of the cask staves.

Recently, however, wood from Limousin and from the state forest of Tronçais – used for ageing cognac – has been embraced due to concern at the extent to which Monlezun has been thinned. In these days of quite proper environmental awareness, it is an arresting thought that 10 mature trees are needed to make each giant oak vat used for blending and ageing these brandies. Results with the lighter oaks are still being assessed.

Armagnac does most of its developing in wood within 20 years but, in any case, after 40 years (cf. 60 years for cognac) it must be transferred to inert glass demijohns or it will spoil. Spirit stops developing when put into glass; a brandy bottled at ten years old, and stored unopened for another five, remains a ten-year-old brandy. Armagnac transferred to demijohns, however, retains the quality-level reached at that stage.

While in cask there is a loss of alcoholic strength of about one degree abv a year, and armagnac, too, loses a share of its distillate to the angels through evaporation. Between Cognac and Armagnac this amounts to about 55,000 bottles every day.

Good armagnacs destined to spend many years of ageing usually pass one or two years in new oak to pick up a lot of wood influence and then doze over much longer stretches in gentler, more benign oak. The techniques of blending and reducing to commercial strength follow broadly the same precepts as in cognac. Distilled water and armagnac, to a strength of about 18% abv, are used to take the spirit down very gradually to 40–43% abv.

The extra dimension with armagnac concerns the two types of spirit from the different stills. Styles can be of any blend between the two generic types, which means that a brand's house-style could be exactly to your taste; but first you have to find it!

## Label information

Most of the label terms, regulations and conventions that apply to armagnac are the same as those of cognac. Descriptions such as VSOP, Extra etc. are used by producers to refer to the quality sequence of their own range and bear only broad relation to what is offered under the same description by their rivals.

This is why the youngest brandies used in a cross-section of VSOPs can vary by as much as 10 years; many armagnac firms want to make their VSOP really outstanding because it accounts for such a big sales sector. Generally speaking, the average age of brandies used in armagnac blends is higher than in cognac and much higher than the legal minima.

| | Legal min. age | Usual min. age | Main parameters |
|---|---|---|---|
| THREE STAR<br>SÉLECTION DE LUXE<br>MONOPOLE<br>VO (VERY OLD) | 2 yrs | 4 yrs | 3–7 yrs |
| VSOP (VERY SPECIAL<br>OLD PALE)<br>RÉSERVE ADC<br>(AIDE DE CAMP) | 4 yrs | 7–8 yrs | 5–15 yrs |
| EXTRA NAPOLÉON<br>XO (EXTRA OLD)<br>EXTRA OLD<br>VIEILLE RÉSERVE<br>(OLD RESERVE)<br>TRÈS VIEILLE<br>(VERY OLD)<br>HORS D'AGE | 5 yrs | 10 yrs | 10–40 yrs |

Proof is required from the producers for claims of age and vintage, and vintage armagnacs must now be at least 10 years-old. The professional body that oversees the brandy has a six-man panel that meets twice a month to sample batches bound for export in parcels of 10 cases or more. If what they examine does not smell and taste the way armagnac should, then the entire batch does not get its export ticket.

*There is a particular emphasis on traditional production methods at Samalens – a number of stills date from the last century.*

## Places to visit

Armagnac is delightfully back-of-beyond country with the ambience and timelessness of Marcel Pagnol's delicious rural trilogy about Fanny, César and Marius. It is tranquil, smiling and reassuring, and gratifyingly unbroached by the outside world. The modern name for the region is Gers, but this is better-known as Gascony, ancient Aquitania, and the capital is the former Gallo-Roman town of Auch with its steep, narrow, medieval lanes (called *pousterles*) and a 'recent' cathedral, begun in the 15th century. Important armagnac brandy towns are Eauze and Nogaro, where cellars may be visited, and the latter has a motor-racing circuit. Condom has an armagnac museum.

Barbotan-les-Thermes was a Roman spa, and Lectoure, with its mansions and religious monuments from the 15th and 16th centuries intact, has been designated a 'city of art'.

The enormously photogenic *bastides* scattered about the countryside are evidence of a tumultuous past. These fortified villages take you back to the times when a visit to the neighbouring village was a major expedition. Among the best are the following: Larressingle, which dates from the 12th century and is also an armagnac firm's business address; Valence-sur-Baïse, which has a fine Cistercian abbey; Montréal, with its arcaded square and pretty lanes; Fources, which still has streets of half-timbered houses, a clock-tower and a medieval castle; and Mirande, which in some ways is very much as it was when pilgrims passed through on the way to Santiago de Compostela.

A number of rivers cross Gers and there are excellent sailing, canoeing and angling centres, such as Marciac and Plaisance. Lakes and reservoirs are well-equipped, as at Masseube, Marsan and Gimont, and there is some fantastic river-rafting on offer at Risole and Lombez.

Travelling south from Gers you will reach the foothills of the Pyrenees, fine walking and horse-riding terrain with a number of interesting caves to visit, some with prehistoric wall-engravings. Lourdes, perhaps the most famous cave, or grotto, in Europe, lies beyond Tarbes in the Hautes Pyrénées region to the south.

Do not be put off going to a bullfight in this part of the world, because they are not in the style of Spanish bullfighting. The *courses landaises* involve frisky young cows in a small arena charging at grinning, show-off youths who, if they are good, can jump over the cow's head, sometimes turning a somersault in the process.

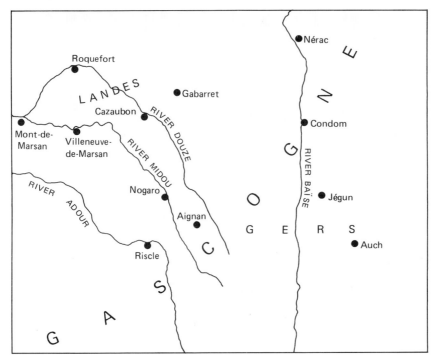

*Armagnac is distilled in the area of the same name in the Gers region of southwest France.*

## LISTINGS

### Casteja

Casteja is named after the head of Borie Manoux, a well-known Bordeaux wine firm with some important classed growths on its books. M. Casteja is a great lover of armagnac and took the opportunity to set up in production himself. The brandies are continuously-distilled in the best area, the Bas Armagnac, and Casteja does the ageing and blending. There are no visitor facilities.

### Labels

*** 3yo; VSOP 6yo; Grande Réserve 10yo; Hors d'Age 15yo.

### CASTEJA GRANDE RÉSERVE

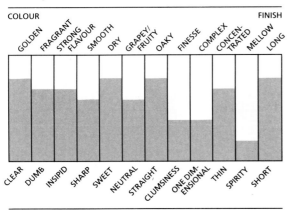

### CASTEJA HORS D'AGE

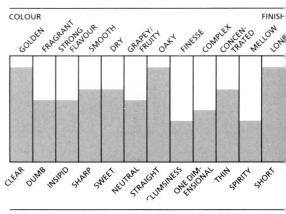

### Château Garreau

A delightfully rural business run with pawky individuality but offering great merit in what the visitor encounters – there isn't a year goes by without M. Garreau's armagnacs winning competition prizes up and down the country.

M. Garreau has 20 hectares of vines on the 80 hectare (198 acres) estate and is presently participating in some distillation and ageing research with the Eauze Departmental Laboratory. His three stills date back to 1912 and his son has just invented a new type with the aid of a state research grant. It is heated by electricity, with an energy saving of 40%, and is regarded as something of a breakthrough. The blending follows a formula

48

which is a family secret and the casks are made of oak from woodland on the estate. There is a little vine growers' museum in a 17th-century barn on the property.

Visitors are welcome; telephone for details.

## Labels

***; Cuvée Royale 5yo; Napoléon; 10-year-old; 15-year-old; 20-year-old.

## Château de Laubade

The property is situated in the Bas Armagnac and the 105 hectare (259 acre) vineyard is the largest in the Armagnac district. Production is about 300000 bottles a year from 1 million litres of wine. Stocks amount to 2000 casks of high-strength spirit, the equivalent of two million bottles. The grapes are principally Ugni Blanc with Baco, Colombard and a healthy 13 hectares (32 acres) of Folle Blanche.

The still is the traditional Armagnacais type and all distillation is complete within a month of the vintage. It is carried out with a light lees in suspension in the wine, giving enhanced flavour to the spirit. All the armagnac spends three years in new oak casks, slightly larger than are used elsewhere, from the local Gascon Forest. The wood is split by hand, which is very unusual these days. The spirit from each grape-type is aged separately and then blended in the proportions required by M. Lesgourgues, the owner. About 40% of production is exported to 30 different countries.

It is a single-property, estate-bottled armagnac and these are the elements M. Lesgourgues wants to present; his range starts at VSOP because he is only interested in selling old armagnac. He offers

Laubade vintages back to 1935, the early years of which are mostly from the Baco grape, as well as a range of vintaged armagnacs from a different property covering 1895 to 1965. There are one or two bottles left of Laubade 1886 at £695 (US$1147) each! M. Lesgourgues also produces a clear, unaged brandy from Folle Blanche only which retains the distinctive and perfumed aroma of the grape. It may not be called armagnac since there is no oak-ageing.

## Labels

VSOP 6yo; Hors d'Age 8–9yo; vintages 1975–1935.

### CHÂTEAU DE LAUBADE VSOP

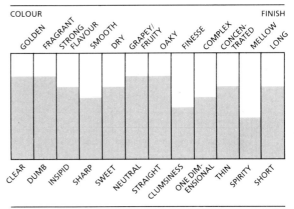

### CHÂTEAU DE LAUBADE HORS D'AGE

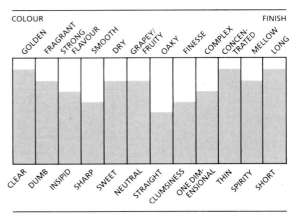

*Very old cognac (60 yrs) and armagnac (40 yrs) are transferred to wicker-covered glass jars called 'carboys'.*

## CHÂTEAU DE LAUBADE 1944

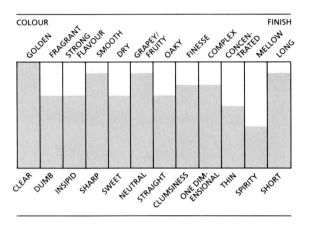

### Château de Malliac

The Malliac name is one of Gascony's oldest, going back to the 12th century. Jehan de Malliac was a Crusader, and the current occupants of his castle are still crusading, this time in the name of armagnac. The present company was established in 1855 and the Bertholon family acquired the Château de Malliac in the early years of this century.

The Malliac approach is a pleasing mix of quality production and light-hearted informal enthusiasm for its brandies and the life-style they represent. Malliac buys spirits from growers with generations of track-record behind them of working with the firm. All the armagnacs spend the latter period of ageing in the 13th-century cellars of the château. It was the Malliac company that introduced the 'Hors d'Age' category to indicate fine spirits that had been aged for 10–20 years.

Malliac is served on Concorde, at the Elysées Palace in Paris and pretty well everywhere that matters for a quality brandy. Its collection of rare vintage armagnacs is possibly the finest available, and it includes the famous 1944 vintage, for which the grapes were being picked as the Allied forces swept through the French countryside towards the end of the Second World War.

The Folle Blanche was the highly aromatic original grape of armagnac (see page 45) and Malliac's rich, liquorice, plummy varietal armagnac is an extraordinary rarity. It is also from a single vineyard in the best area of Bas Armagnac and vintaged; only a few hundred bottles are possible each year. Ultimate is a blend of the best years of the century. All the vintage brandies carry the year of bottling to indicate when the maturation process ended.

### Labels

VS 2–3yo; VSOP 5–10yo; Napoléon 6–12yo; XO 6–15yo; Hors d'Age Extra 5–20yo; Folle Blanche Varietal 20+yo; Vintages; Ultimate.

## CHÂTEAU DE MALLIAC NAPOLÉON

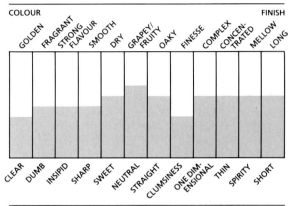

## CHÂTEAU DE MALLIAC HORS D'AGE EXTRA

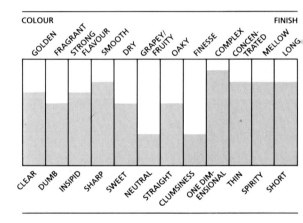

## CHÂTEAU DE MALLIAC FOLLE BLANCHE 1966

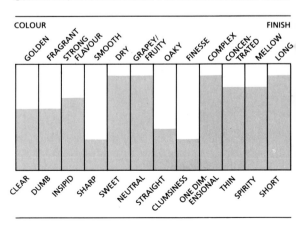

## Château de Sandemagnan

An interesting property and product owned by a well-known restaurateur. M. Guérard grows Ugni Blanc, Folle Blanche and Colombard grapes in his Bas Armagnac vineyard and produces about 30 000 litres of armagnac a year. The bottling is done *in situ* so in every sense this is a single-vineyard, château-bottled armagnac. His still is the traditional continuous Armagnacais type and the spirits are aged in Limousin oak until they take on an attractive amber shade from the wood.

Visitors are catered for on an 'office hours' basis – weekdays 8am until 6pm with two hours off for lunch.

### HORS D'AGE 1240

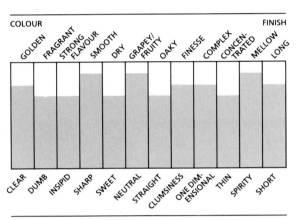

## Clés des Ducs

This is one of a number of armagnac firms which came on to the export markets in the 1970s and achieved restricted brand status. Clés des Ducs is the top-selling brand in France and, as such, concentrates on producing cheaper young armagnac to meet volume sales requirements. Most of its distillation wines, however, do come from the top two production zones. It also has access to a range of vintage brandies.

### Labels
\*\*\*; VSOP 4yo; XO 14–15yo; Extra Grande Réserve 21yo; some vintages.

### CLÉS DES DUCS VSOP

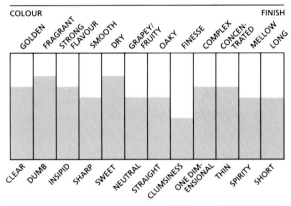

## Darroze

This firm produces a wide range of single vintages and single-estate armagnacs. M. Darroze is a dealer in armagnac but he does so much towards the evolution and formation of the brandies he sells that he is their real creator. He buys old armagnac and young spirit from a network of small individual properties and has a strict and elaborate maturation routine that is applied to them all. They are all distilled absolutely to traditional precepts and are totally natural with nothing added at any stage.

He even has separate cellars with different atmospheres, one damp and one dry. This is not unique in Armagnac but it is very rare, and shows how much attention to detail can go into the preparation of a fine brandy.

All of the armagnacs go into new oak, then older, used oak, and none is sold before ten years of age. Every one of his armagnacs is a vintaged single-estate product.

### Domaine de la Boubée

The Ladevèze family were producing wines on their own domaine at La Boubée before the French Revolution and today 27 hectares (66 acres) of vines are worked for armagnac-production. The firm has Folle Blanche, Ugni Blanc, Colombard and Plant de Graisse grapes, and it is the last major vineyard in Armagnac where the grapes are hand picked at vintage time. Its brandies tend to do well in the various competitions that take place in France. La Boubée is situated in the Ténarèze, the middle-quality zone. The company exports to Britain, Germany and Japan.

### Labels
***; VSOP; Hors d'Age 12yo.

### DOMAINE DE LA BOUBÉE HORS D'AGE

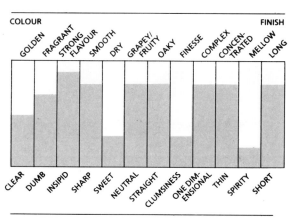

### Dupeyron

The firm owns an extraordinary collection of old and vintage armagnacs, some dating from 1850, which they sell to private individuals, restaurants and specialist outlets in France, Europe and the Far East. It is based in Condom in Armagnac, but also runs an attractive armagnac boutique in a protected building in Paris and a mail-order service.

The company was founded by Joseph Dupeyron in 1905, the Ryst side of the modern firm coming in through the marriage of a grand-daughter in 1945. Today, Jacques Ryst feels that his way of doing business defends the integrity of the product and gives him the commercial liberty that he needs. He seeks out casks of old armagnac for bottling as blends or as single vintages; the range is called Armagnac du Collectionneur. For customers prepared to wait 18 months, he will make up special blends.

Only traditionally-distilled armagnacs from Bas Armagnac and Ténarèze are handled, many of them produced from Folle Blanche grapes, and they are all aged in traditional, but now scarce, local black oak from Monlézun. Sales are around 200 000 bottles a year.

During the summer months there are organized visits at Condom, conducted in four languages, which end with tasting. Visitors are given a connoisseur's diploma.

### Labels
XO; Hors d'Age; Vintages 1976–1904.

### DUPEYRON 1905 VINTAGE

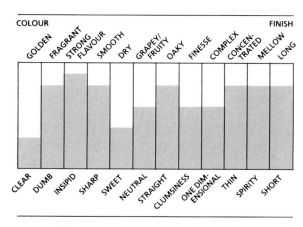

### Janneau

Janneau is the leading exporter of armagnac and does well in the three main foreign trade areas – Europe, North America and the Far East. The better qualities in the Janneau range now account for over 60% of the company's sales. During the 1970s, Janneau sold 45% of the company to Martell to gain the benefits of its promotional power and distribution range, but the family still retains overall control.

Janneau uses both types of still, mainly to help meet volume requirements for Tradition, their *** brand, which is a blend of the two styles of spirit. VSOP also has some pot-still distillate, but the higher categories are wholly from traditional stills. The family still have vineyards at the Domaine de Mouchac estate, and from it they produce a single-property armagnac, usually vintaged.

The company was founded in 1851 and, with five generations' growth, the Janneau stocks of old armagnac are impressive – the equivalent of almost five million bottles. Etienne Janneau is a tireless proselytiser around the world on behalf of armagnac and a great campaigner against the misuse of valuable medium-aged stocks to gain sales by undercutting cognac in price.

Visitors are welcome.

## Labels

Tradition 4yo; VSOP 10yo; Napoléon 12yo; XO 15yo; Some vintages; Domaine de Mouchac is single-estate.

## JANNEAU VSOP

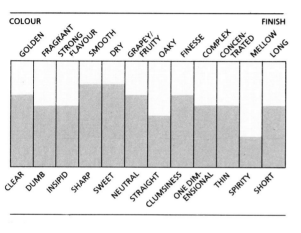

## Larressingle

The brand is named after the 13th-century château and vineyards bought in 1896 by Gabriel Papelorey. He continued the armagnac business begun by his father in 1837 and it was the first firm to sell armagnac in bottle rather than in cask. For the range it offers today, it buys in spirit from independent growers around the district and merges them with old armagnacs drawn from its own aged reserves at the château.

The Château de Larressingle is a perfect example of the medieval hamlets that used to cluster close to castles for protection. The better types, of which Larressingle is one, were built integral to the château with access by narrow alleys for security. It was built by the Bishops of Condom in 1250 and is now a protected monument. Exports cover a wide area, with Britain and the United States at the forefront.

## Labels

VSOP 8yo; XO Grande Réserve 15yo.

## LARRESSINGLE VSOP

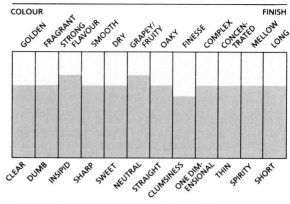

## LARRESSINGLE XO GRANDE RÉSERVE

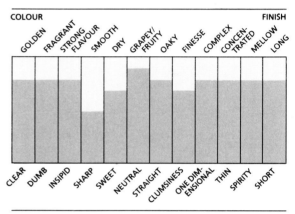

## Marquis de Caussade

The first bottle of armagnac to enter the United States did so in 1934, and it was from the distillery of the Marquis de Caussade. The man who took it there on the maiden voyage of the liner the *Normandie* was the Marquis himself, a member of a long-established noble family who had furnished many musketeers for the French king. The brand was later acquired by a large co-operative and made inroads in several markets, but ten years ago it almost foundered. The present owners combine a full brand operation and a single-vintage business, making good use of the enormous stocks of old brandy in the cellars.

Visitors are welcome.

## Labels

***; VSOP 10yo; Napoléon 12yo; XO 14yo; Vintage range.

## MARQUIS DE CAUSSADE XO

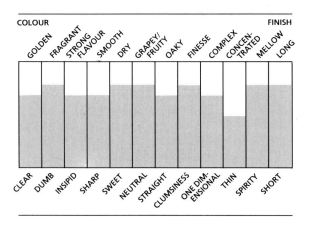

| COLOUR | | | | | | | | | | | FINISH |
| GOLDEN | FRAGRANT | STRONG FLAVOUR | SMOOTH | DRY | GRAPEY/ FRUITY | OAKY | FINESSE | COMPLEX | CONCEN- TRATED | MELLOW | LONG |
|---|---|---|---|---|---|---|---|---|---|---|---|
| CLEAR | DUMB | INSIPID | SHARP | SWEET | NEUTRAL | STRAIGHT | CLUMSINESS | ONE DIM- ENSIONAL | THIN | SPIRITY | SHORT |

### Marquis de Montesquiou

If armagnac is the brandy of d'Artagnan, this is where it touches base because the Montesquious are the descendants of Charles de Batz Castelmore, captain of the Compagnie des Mousquetaires and d'Artagnan of the famous adventure story.

In 1936, Pierre, Marquis de Montesquiou, set up the company to find markets for armagnac that he was having distilled on his estate. It did quite well in France and then in the 1970s it was one of a number of armagnac brands that gained some sales momentum outside France, unfortunately by being promoted as a cheap alternative to cognac.

Montesquiou has vineyards in the Bas Armagnac area, but it also buys in wines which it distils in Armagnacais stills and ages itself. After the spirit comes out of new wood it spends an intermediate period in youngish, used oak before being moved on to the casks in which it will do its main ageing. There are 3700 barrels in the Montesquiou cellars.

### Labels

Monopole *** 3yo; VSOP 5yo; Napoléon 8yo; XO 12yo. Some vintages.

### Marquis de Puységur

This is one of the most successful brands on the export market and does particularly well in duty-free outlets. It has, however, lost much of its individuality by being part of a group of brands which is owned by the cognac firm Camus.

### Labels

***; VSOP; Sélection Privée. Some vintages.

### Samalens

The firm was founded in 1882 and there is a heavy emphasis on the time-honoured ways of doing things; four of the eight stills date from the last century. They are the traditional continuous stills and produce such distinctive spirit that the company's master-distiller can recognize the distillate from each by taste.

The other four stills are pot apparatus requiring double-distillation. The pot-still spirit is only used in the VSOP brandy, and then only to 30% proportion. Ageing is carried out in local black oak from Monlézun. About 69% of sales are abroad, in all five continents.

Visitors are welcome; telephone for information.

### Labels

VSOP; Napoléon; Réserve Impériale XO; Rélique d'Age Inconnu; Vieille Rélique; Rélique Ancestrale 15yo in glass and pewter; Cristal Rélique; Rélique du Siècle 100yo (i.e. 70 years in oak, then transferred to glass demijohns in 1957) Limited to 100 units. The last two are in Baccarat decanters; all are from the Bas Armagnac.

## RÉLIQUE D'AGE INCONNU

| COLOUR | | | | | | | | | | | FINISH |
| GOLDEN | FRAGRANT | STRONG FLAVOUR | SMOOTH | DRY | GRAPEY/ FRUITY | OAKY | FINESSE | COMPLEX | CONCEN- TRATED | MELLOW | LONG |
|---|---|---|---|---|---|---|---|---|---|---|---|
| CLEAR | DUMB | INSIPID | SHARP | SWEET | NEUTRAL | STRAIGHT | CLUMSINESS | ONE DIM- ENSIONAL | THIN | SPIRITY | SHORT |

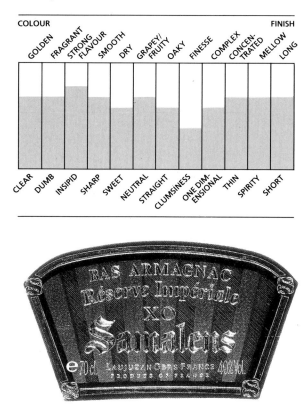

*Samalens ages its Bas-Armagnac brandy in black oak.*

## RÉLIQUE ANCESTRALE 15 YEARS-OLD

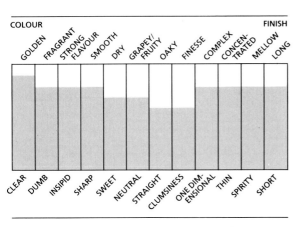

## CRISTAL RÉLIQUE

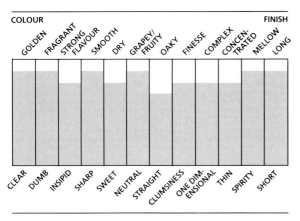

## RÉLIQUE DU SIÈCLE

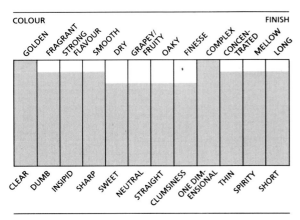

## Sempé

Henri-Abel Sempé set up his company just two years before the outbreak of the Second World War, during which he was very active in the French underground – he was later decorated by the British government for his exploits. M. Sempé's armagnac, too, has been decorated; the 1965 vintage received the Grand Prix du Président de la République!

Sempé is still a grower, distiller and blender but most of the wine-making and distilling for the volume of brandy the company needs is done by well-established independents. Most of the spirit is traditionally-produced and matures in local Monlézun oak.

### Labels

Fine 3yo; VSOP 6yo; Napoléon 8yo; Extra 10yo. Some vintages.

## SEMPÉ VSOP

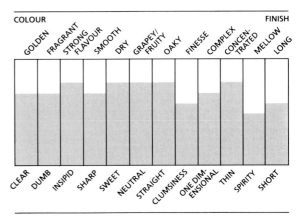

# GRAPE BRANDY – FINES

A *fine* is generally the name given to a high-quality grape brandy and particularly to the regulated brandies from specific regions of France other than cognac and armagnac. These tend not to be well-known outside their areas of production, but three of them have a certain celebrity, if only because of the famous wine names incorporated in their official denomination.

*Fine de Bordeaux* is produced from wines grown within the enormous area delimited for the Bordeaux, or claret, appellation. Confusingly, however, the wines involved are not from claret, or white bordeaux, grapes, but from the cognac grapes Ugni Blanc and Colombard. Indeed, the whole production is based on cognac, with double-distillation in

*To ensure uniformity in production, it is necessary to monitor the spirit carefully at every stage in the distillation process.*

# GRAPE BRANDY – FRENCH BRANDY

The use of the words 'French Brandy' here is meant more precisely than may at first be obvious. Under the main category heading of Grape Brandy, the principal types (cognac, armagnac and the various fines) have been delineated and you will have noticed that they take their names from their geographic origins.

The rest of the grape brandy produced in France has no special name-entitlement or geographic requirement placed upon it, and the only practical term left to describe it is the simple, general one of 'brandy'. There is no great market within France for this kind of product, so use of 'eau-de-vie de vin' would be inappropriate. Thus the convention of 'French Brandy' has come to indicate spirit distilled from grapes from any French vineyards other than those entitled to a protected eau-de-vie appellation.

Since most French Brandy is sold abroad the term works well, perhaps too well, because many of the people who buy it in, for example, the UK and the US probably believe that it is some kind of cognac. "If it is French and it is brandy it must be cognac" is the reasoning, often underpinned by the brand-owning firm's having a Cognac address printed on the label.

French Brandy is usually made from different eaux-de-vie bought from the French state alcohol monopoly. These spirits derive from vineyards all over the country and from numerous grape varieties, and are produced in continuous stills.

Brand-owning firms buy the types and ages they need in order to blend their own house-styles, similarly, in fact, to the cognac companies, but on a much shorter time-scale. Some spirits are combined with varying quantities of cognac and other brandies to lend flavour. The blends spend varying periods in wood depending upon which markets they will eventually reach – traditionally the UK has required three years' maturation, the US two.

The better French Brandies are quite wholesome products, with good grapey flavours and smooth finish. They lack depth, concentration or any individualism, but for their target markets this is no drawback. They are consistent from year to year and pitch their prices carefully to be as attractive as possible against the starter prices for cognac.

Many of the brands belong, through subsidiaries, to cognac firms – the rationale being that

pot-stills required, coming off at 72% abv maximum. Not surprisingly the finished brandy is a close cousin to cognac in broad style, flavour and aroma. Some is aged for quite long periods in oak, the choice being that of the producer since no specific requirement is made in the regulations.

*Fine de Bourgogne* must derive from wines made from the authorized Burgundy grapes which have been grown within the appellation controlée zone. It is variable in quality, from young and coarse to mature and mellow, but is rare to encounter outside its home ground.

Regulated grape brandy from the champagne-producing area cannot be called 'Fine de Champagne' since it would be confused with Cognac's Fine Champagne designation. Consequently, the more clumsy and oblique name of *Fine de la Marne* renders almost incognito this brandy made from wines produced from Champagne grapes, grown within the appellation contrôlée zone.

So little is made now that the entire production comes from a single firm, Goyard, in the champagne town of Ay. In their distillation of the fine, they also include the lees-rich wine that is disgorged from bottles of champagne. This gives extra flavour to the light and elegant brandy which is made by the *calandre* system (see 'Marc' below).

In addition to the above, fines are mostly from the same areas that produce the marcs mentioned below.

## Some Producers
Château d'Arley; Romanée Conti; Mommessin; Pupillon; Roulot; Drouhin; Goyard.

the firms would still like to have the business of those who choose, for whatever reason, not to buy cognac.

At present these brandies have free use of terms such as VSOP, Napoléon etc. to further the associations – and confusion – with cognac, but this may soon be ended by new legislation that is currently being planned.

World sales are around the 3¼ million case mark (40 million bottles). There is little interest in the product in France itself and most is made for export; the leading brand exports 98% of its production.

## Raynal Three Barrels

This is the biggest-selling non-appellation controlée grape brandy from France and is produced from spirits from continuous stills. It is very approachable and smooth in style, not unlike many of the lighter breeds of Californian and Australian brandies.

The brandies are aged in oak and their blending seeks to impart a 'Frenchness' to the brand. The product's absolute consistency from year to year, of course, largely stems from the uniformity of the high-strength spirits used in its manufacture. The dual description of the brand as both VSOP and Napoléon underlines how meaningless these terms are if not used properly although, to an unpractised eye, they no doubt underline the 'French brandy-ness' of the product.

The company was set up towards the end of last century and became part of the Moët-Hennessy group in 1974. The brand is expanding; sales total 650 000 cases a year and divide about equally between Britain, the United States and other foreign markets.

### RAYNAL/THREE BARRELS VSOP NAPOLÉON

| COLOUR | | | | | | | | | | | FINISH |
|--------|--|--|--|--|--|--|--|--|--|--|--------|
| GOLDEN | FRAGRANT | STRONG FLAVOUR | SMOOTH | DRY | GRAPEY/ FRUITY | OAKY | FINESSE | COMPLEX | CONCEN- TRATED | MELLOW | LONG |
| CLEAR | DUMB | INSIPID | SHARP | SWEET | NEUTRAL | STRAIGHT | CLUMSINESS | ONE DIM- ENSIONAL | THIN | SPIRITY | SHORT |

# POMACE BRANDY – MARC

In France, marc is the name given to the plant residues left behind after the grapes have been pressed and the juice run off to be fermented into wine. This mass of grape skins, stalks, pips and pulp (known as pomace in English) is also fermentable and when the results are distilled the product is called marc brandy.

Although enthusiasts have brought about some activity in assorted markets, French marc has remained essentially a local drink produced with some variations from district to district in France. Its Italian counterpart, grappa, has this same simple, artisanal production level, but also has a more sophisticated product that is exported widely.

### Distillation

One distinctive traditional method of distilling marc is the calandre, a multi-chamber still through which steam is passed. The pomace lies on internal plates and the pressurized steam extracts its alcohol before moving on to a rectification column where the vapours are further concentrated. Each chamber may be isolated while the others continue to function so that spent pomace may be removed and fresh supplies loaded without interrupting the distillation operation. Other marcs are produced using both pot- and continuous stills.

Travelling distillers are still used in some places, but most of the distillation is done centrally by two or three specialist firms.

### The brandy

Marcs are usually an acquired taste, with their forthright earthiness and oily aromas. Deep fruit flavour and carbide bouquet can be uneasy extremes to reconcile, but these are brandies that foster great loyalty.

*Marc de Bourgogne* is the best-known and is made from pomace from the Burgundy production zone, often from the top wine estates. If derived from a single appellation, e.g. Montrachet, Chambertin etc., the name may appear on the label. Marc de Bourgogne tends to be smooth, light (by virtue of there being no stalks in the pomace) and full in flavour due to the low distillation strength of 52% abv.

*Marc de Champagne* is made from grapes grown within the champagne-production area.

These and marcs from Aquitaine, Centre-Est, Franche-Comté, Bugey, Savoie, Auvergne,

*Etienne Brana, a Basque, produces a marc which is rated very highly by French gourmet magazines.*

Coteaux de la Loire, Côtes du Rhone, Provence, Languedoc, Alsace (for Gewürztraminer) and Lorraine have their names protected and their production regulated by law. They all must pass examination by tasting panels.

Most marcs are aged in oak for three to 10 years.

## LISTINGS

### Brana, Etienne

Etienne Brana is a proud Basque winemaker and distiller, and the universe in which he places himself does not acknowledge political details like the French/Spanish border. His competitive benchmarks include Rioja and Navarra in Spain as well as Jurançon and Madiran in France. His artisanal distillation includes marc from the pomace of Irouléguy, a Basque wine from a tiny production area, and pear, plum and raspberry eaux-de-vie.

The marc is made from Tannat, Cabernets Sauvignon and Franc, and Aoce d'Irouléguy, the grape-mix of the Irouléguy wine made by the local co-operative. The brandy achieves an aroma of very ripe grapes and secondary fragrances of almonds and preserved fruit. Brana's brandies are very highly thought of and assorted French gourmet magazines, including *Gault Millau*, regularly write well of them.

Brana built his distillery in 1974, the same year as he planted his pear-trees, and the fruit he uses today for his brandies comes only from that orchard. From 1991, the 14 hectares of vines he planted in 1987 will begin producing wine – and the marc, like the fruit brandies, will become a single-property product.

*Marc d'Irouléguy has an aroma of very ripe grapes.*

## Other producers

Among brands exported are: Château d'Arlay; Grivelet; Lejay-Legoute; Papillon; Bouchard; Caves des Hautes Côtes; Château de Pommard; Mommessin; Romanée Conti; Boudier; Ponnelle; Reine Pédauque; Briottet; Drouhin; Chevalier; and Domaine des Hautes Cornières.

## MARC D'IROULÉGUY

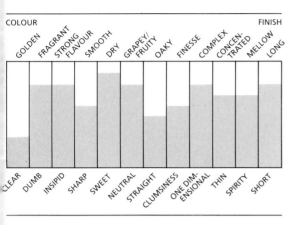

*In the past, bouilleurs moved portable stills from site to site.*

# FRUIT BRANDY

The origins of fruit brandy stem from one of the numerous cholera epidemics that still swept various parts of Europe from time to time in the 17th century. At that time distillation was a medical/alchemical activity and, around 1650, a practitioner-monk had the idea of distilling a cherry potion as a remedy for the disease.

Irrespective of its success or failure as such, the idea spread during the rest of the century, particularly into regions where there was little or no wine-making tradition. Since the 14th century, many European convents and monasteries had had primitive stills which they used to make elixirs and draughts from wine and aromatic herbs.

Since the distilling of cherry spirit expanded rapidly in German-speaking areas, Kirsch (or Kirschwasser) was the commonest description applied to it, but soon other fruits were being fermented and distilled, in particular mirabelle and quetsch plums, and, more recently, the William pear.

All of the fruit used grew wild, of course, and it was only with the establishing of each new spirit flavour that orchards and plantations were created. Raspberry spirit (framboise) was rare when it was first introduced in the 20th century, but today most types of what were once wild berries are distilled into fruit brandy. Even holly berry brandy can be made – it is very rare indeed, but what style for Christmas toasting!

Among the fruits now distilled into brandy in France are Golden Delicious apples, but by far the most famous French apple (cider) brandy is calvados from Normandy.

# FRUIT BRANDY – CALVADOS

Calvados is an apple, or cider, brandy, protected by its own appellations just as are grape brandies. It takes its name from the département of Calvados in Normandy, north-west France, itself named after an invading Spanish Armada galleon, *El Calvador*, which foundered on the rocky coast there.

Normandy is a mixed landscape of treeless prairie, rich pasture meadows, orchards and stone-built towns. There have always been apple trees in Normandy, and people had long made cider before the first documented reference to apple brandy in 1553.

## Vineyard zones

Strictly speaking, calvados may be made from apples or pears, but it is as an apple brandy that it is best known. The original appellation contrôlée designation applies to the heartland of the production area, the Pays d'Auge, and this is still regarded as the source of the best-quality calvados. The full designation is 'calvados du Pays d'Auge'.

The second-ranking calvados are also appellations contrôlées and derive from the zones surrounding the Pays d'Auge heartland. They are: Avranchin; Mortainais; Calvados; Pays de Bray; Cotentin; Pays du Merlerault; Domfrontais; Perche; Pays de la Risle; and Vallée de l'Orne. Again, each of these geographic names must appear with the brandy name, calvados, and each spirit must be unblended and wholly from the stated zone.

There is also a lesser brandy appellation with the long-winded name 'eau-de-vie de cidre de Normandie' which may be made from ciders from any part of Normandy.

Calvados now has sufficiently good distribution in export markets to be no longer the esoteric product it once was. After a short promotional campaign in the UK, sales doubled in 1988. It also has a notable presence in the US and German markets after years of quietly building volume.

Over 48 types of apple qualify to be made into calvados and these are graded from sweet to tart. Fermentation is by the natural yeasts on the skins and, after pulping, should take a month, except for 'Pays d'Auge' calvados which takes six weeks.

## Distillation and maturation

The main difference between the two appellations is that Pays d'Auge cider is double-distilled in a Charentais (Cognac) pot-still, while the others are converted in a continuous still.

As in the case of other brandies, there is more substance and flavour to a pot-still calvados, and it will show more complexity, nuance and roundness. Continuous still calvados is lighter and smoother.

New calvados spirit goes into new oak casks and the tannin-transfer from the wood into the brandy gives it body and colour. It is then moved into a used cask whose influences are gentler and more gradual.

Most calvados is drunk in France at two to three years old, but exports – about 30% of sales – tend to be aged to about six/seven years and more. An age may be declared on the label and will refer to the youngest brandy in the blend.

Characteristics vary quite a bit between the young and the more mature styles, and the 'best' is a matter of personal choice. Certainly the older styles – from VSOP upwards – are immensely attractive, showing breed, smoothness and good length. The following conventional terms are used on labels:

| | |
|---|---|
| THREE STARS | Average 2 years' oak ageing |
| VIEUX or RÉSERVE | Average 3 years' oak ageing |
| VO or VSOP or VIEILLE RÉSERVE } | Average 4 years' oak ageing |
| EXTRA or NAPOLÉON or HORS D'AGE or AGE INCONNU } | Average 6 years' or more oak ageing |

All calvados must taste and smell in accordance with the generic nature of the product while still leaving scope for individual brand- or house-styles, and a tasting panel assesses samples of every batch of brandy made prior to its going on sale. Bottle-strength is 40–45% abv.

Calvados of different ages are blended to produce final brandies, and these are 'rested' for a number of months to 'marry'. Some distillers exchange brandies to extend this principle or pool supplies to create enough volume to sustain a brand. This must be done within the production zone in order to retain the appellation.

The calvados version of a single-property brandy is a bottle with the words *production fermière* or *produit fermier* on the label. It essentially means that, from orchard to bottling, the farmer has produced the brandy using unhurried, artisanal methods – the brandy equivalent of home-cooking.

There used to be a punctuation point during grand dinners in Normandy called *le trou normand*. At a certain stage in a meal a shot of calvados was served to zest up the guests' metabolism and also pave the way for the courses to come. *Trou* means 'hole' in French and the brandy did indeed seem to create space to accommodate the rest of the meal.

## Other producers

Arc de Triomphe; Berneroy; Bon Esprit; Boulard; Busnel; Camut; Château La Boise; Coquerel; Courcel; Fiefs Sainte Anne; Ducs de Normandie; Gilbert; Groult; Montarcy; Morin; Morice; Père Magloire; Salas; Un Trou Normand.

## Places to visit

Mont Saint-Michel has a fantastic setting, a whole village fitting on to a great off-shore rock, with probably the steepest main street in the world and a medieval Gothic abbey at its end. If you are out on the great flat sands when you hear the siren, get back to higher ground because the tide can come in at the speed of a galloping horse.

There is another Gothic building, this time a cathedral, at Bayeux, where you can walk along the 70 metres (230 ft) of the famous Romanesque tapestry woven by Queen Mathilde, which recounts the story of William the Conqueror's invasion of England and his victory at the Battle of Hastings. Nearby are the D-Day Landing beaches and the military cemeteries associated with 6 June, 1944. Caen has a Memorial Museum with memorabilia of the Battle of Normandy.

There are horse-training demonstrations and driving competitions at the Haras du Pin, created by Louis XIV, and the Normandy-Maine National Park has 200 000 hectares (494 193 acres) of beautiful copses, meadows and wooded hills. Coastal Granville is a former privateer town with ramparts to prove it, and at Mardi Gras it holds a

*In addition to protecting the product, the bottling of brandy, first introduced in the nineteenth century, serves to halt the maturing process.*

four-day Fishermen's Carnival. Ferry-boats leave from there for the peaceful Chausey Islands.

Honfleur is very pretty and is popular with visiting painters. Canada's first explorers set off from here in the 17th century; yachts still fill the harbour today and you can buy hot shrimps on the quays. Sainte Catherine's Church is built in the shape of an upturned boat's hull.

Deauville and Trouville have long been fashionable resorts for Parisians and the casino, the horse-racing and the polo have stayed on to remind us of those *fin de siècle* times. Today wind-surfers, golfers and walkers also enjoy the elegant surroundings.

Manor houses and stud farms dot the landscape and many of the coastal resorts offer thalassotherapy facilities. This is a very French form of therapy which involves cossetting the body with various seawater treatments.

Cabourg is a rival resort to Deauville and was 'Balbec' in Proust's novel *A la Recherche du Temps Perdu*.

## BOULARD FINE CALVADOS

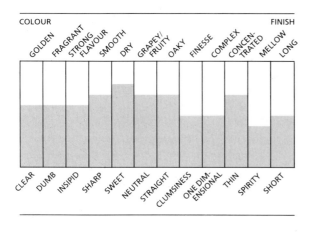

Bagnoles de l'Orne is a spa town dating from the middle ages. It has the special old-fashioned charm and atmosphere usually encountered in nineteenth century spa resorts, whether in France, or elsewhere in Europe.

The Normans were great builders of ships, churches and castles. The architectural style of their churches, generally known in Britain as 'Norman', is described in Normandy and elsewhere as 'Romanesque'. The castle builders were particularly innovative, and a vast, drum-towered 13th century Château Gaillard on the banks of the Seine was the prototype for castle-building throughout Europe for the next five centuries.

## PÈRE MAGLOIRE GRANDE FINE XSOP

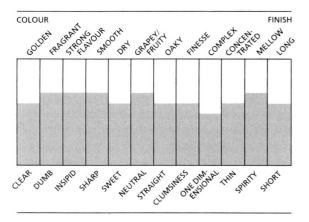

# FRUIT BRANDY – NAMED FRUIT BRANDY

Over 4 million bottles of fruit brandy are drunk in France each year, over half of which is from William pears. About three-quarters of a million bottles are exported, most of them to West Germany, Benelux and Italy, but a fifth goes to the US and Canada. The production is still essentially a cottage industry with most of the distilleries employing fewer than 10 people. The great merit of this is that the brandies are wholly hand-crafted, getting the most out of the raw materials in terms of aroma and flavour.

It also means that the production regulations are based on these slow, traditional methods, and have now enshrined them as standard. It is not so very long ago that these methods were still being handed down orally from generation to generation. The only raw material is the fruit – there are no additives of any kind, natural or synthetic, no chaptalization – and it takes, for example, 28 kg (62 lb) of William pears to make 1 litre of pure alcohol spirit.

Most fruit brandy production takes place in Alsace, in north-east France, but small amounts are also made in Franche-Comté, the Rhône and Loire valleys and the south-west.

## The fruits

These divide into three categories and are treated in two different ways. Stone and pip fruits go into vats for fermentation, while berries, which have a low natural sugar content, are first macerated in alcohol.

The weight of the stone fruits and pears in the vat produces a free-run (i.e. no mechanical pressing) juice which ferments with the natural yeasts on their skins. Most of the sugar is converted into alcohol in about 10 days, but fermentation may take six weeks to complete.

Berries would produce very little alcohol from their own sugar-content, so they are macerated in fruit spirit for at least a month at the rate of 25 litres of 50% abv spirit for every 100 kg (220 lb) of fruit. Gentle fermentation occurs during this period, but it is nothing like the more vigorous fermentation which occurs with stone fruit. The resulting mixture is distilled in a single operation.

*Maturing cognac can lose as much as 3% per year of its volume through evaporation. The regular loss is made good by topping up the casks, ideally with the same brandy.*

## Distillation

Copper stills over a naked flame or double-walled boilers are used for distillation. The latter allows steam to circulate in the gap between the walls until the vapours pass over. An artisanal aspect of the operation is the tasting of the running spirit to identify heads, heart and tails, instead of using a hydrometer. Still-strength is 50–60% abv and the distillate goes into glass or stoneware demijohns.

These traditional routines indicate the way that distillers are accustomed to making their fruit brandy. The closely-detailed legislation by the French authorities is based on what the fruit-brandy makers were already doing. If the laws had required changes or compromises, the chances are that these conservative distillers would have ignored them in order to maintain their product in the form they had long known and valued.

## Maturation

Maturation of fruit brandies follows precisely the old routines used when quantities were appropriate to a family supply, but now that even modest commercial volume is needed, the large scale can be a problem. As a result, vast attics have had to be built under tile roofs to replicate the loft in a single farmhouse, with its wide temperature variations, where the brandies were usually stored.

At the start, the demijohns are left open to allow volatile elements to drift off, and they are stored away from light. The inert glass allows the spirit to settle and mellow while retaining its pure, clean flavour with no input of any kind. Some brandies – among them those from plums – do better in casks of spent oak or ash, which is very hard and white. The spirits soften and take on body during at least a year's minimum ageing; any longer will depend on the distiller's house-style.

Mirabelle brandy is usually aged for two or three years, William pear for up to five years, quetsch for eight to ten years and kirsch often longer than ten years.

## Some producers

Bertrand; Cusenier; Les Distillateurs Réunis; Dolfi; Gisselbrecht; Goulby; Hacquard; Holl; Larrière; Laurent; Lehmann; Lemercier; Massènez; Nuss-bäumer; Sainte Odile; Sipp; Preiss; Wolfberger; Witz.

# SPANISH

Spanish brandy has been around for a long time, its pedigree going back to the Moors who occupied the Iberian peninsula for seven centuries until 1492. Since distillation skills are thought to have worked their way gradually north into the heart of Europe, it would seem fair to assume that they were practised south of the Pyrenees, to some degree at least, well before they filtered into France.

Grape brandy is a very popular drink in Spain and the vast majority of it is produced in Jerez by the famous sherry-making firms. Sherry is a complex, carefully-structured wine, with several different and complicated treatments involved before the resulting wines are finally blended in precise proportions, and it is interesting to note that something of the same approach is used in making Spanish brandy.

No other brandy-producing industry gives itself so much control over the end result, enabling the distillers and blenders to hone and fine-tune flavours and aromas to an extraordinary degree. They do not simply crimp or temper the fringes of a brandy's natural characteristics as the still delivers them; with their skills and techniques they can actually build brandy styles layer by layer.

The exceptions to the Jerez monopoly are from the Penedés district of Cataluña in the north-east of Spain, best-known for Cava champagne-method sparkling wines, and one or two other isolated operations. Two firms in Penedés, Mascaro and Torres, have followed the broad principles of cognac production, but have adapted them to produce very attractive, high-quality brandy.

*There have been Spanish vineyards since the time of the Phoenicians, and today Spain devotes a greater proportion of land to viticulture than any other country.*

## GRAPE BRANDY – JEREZ

In the south of Spain, where the coast has turned the corner west of Gibraltar's tilted slab and rises towards the Portuguese border, lie the sherry towns of Jerez, Puerto Santa María and Cádiz. They are very ancient, dating from about 1000 BC, and have long been strategically important for both trading and making war. Together with Sanlucar de Barrameda, they comprise the principal wine-trade towns of the Jerez region.

Over the centuries, Greeks, Carthaginians, Romans, Visigoths and Moors settled the Cádiz coast and points inland. Although the Muslim Moors may well not have been consumers of wine or *aqua vitae*, they certainly tended vineyards, and many continued to do so after the Reconquista.

Apart from the sea, there are two important rivers – the Guadalquivir and the Guadalete – which have influenced both the microclimate in which the grapes grow and the traffic which, over the centuries, has passed through Jerez.

Seville, upriver on the Guadalquivir, has long been a great administrative and cultural centre, and was the departure point for many of the expeditions to the Americas, and Columbus's flagship for one of them, the *Santa Maria*, was built in, and named after, Puerto Santa María.

*Like cognac, Mascaró brandies are aged in Limousin oak.*

### The brandy

Jerez brandy is highly original in its manufacture, a result of the dexterity and flexibility of the wine-makers and distillers through their long experience of making fortified sherry wines. This has given the brandy-makers a range of raw spirit characteristics to choose from, and a very special wood-ageing technique not used elsewhere.

Notwithstanding the wide range of house-styles, from light to quite full and sumptuous, the broad generic character of Jerez brandy has a softer, rounder feel to it without losing the typical brandy bite. Historically it has been regarded as very sweet and caramelly, particularly to Anglo-Saxon tastes, and although caramel is added, much of its sweetness derives naturally from the fibres of the oak wood in which it is aged.

Today it can have a very rich texture, but is not nearly as sweet as it used to be. The flavour is well-stated yet elegant and in general Jerez brandy is less austerely dry than cognac. Indeed, it probably offers better reliability than its French high-volume counterparts, especially in the middle to upper quality levels; only the absolute top-of-the-range cognacs and armagnacs will outshine the best of Spanish brandies. Of the two French brandies, armagnac is in fact the one with which comparison is more valid.

A century ago, the Jerez approach to brandy-making was closely based on that of Cognac, but Spanish taste has evolved the brandy's broad generic style away from that of cognac. There are still close links between the two towns, but from precepts initially common to them, the brandy-makers in the two countries now aspire to different ends.

Spaniards drink a lot of brandy – about 9 million cases of home brands a year, plus imports – and it has been the most popular spirit in Spain for the past 20 years. They export another 1¼ million cases to over 75 different countries, but largely to Spanish-speaking Latin America – and it could have been four times that figure if one particularly successful producer had not actually gone to Mexico and set up a distillery on the spot.

Exports have increased sevenfold since 1960. Domecq is to Spanish brandy as Hennessy is to cognac, and the Presidente brand produced *in situ* in Mexico is the world's biggest seller, turning over four million cases each year.

### The countryside

Spain is a country of panoramic landscapes and big, luminous skies, but one of the first sights to register with visitors as they drive between towns is the large, black, anatomically correct silhouettes of bulls planted atop every other roadside knoll. These are the advertising hoardings of Osborne (pronounce the final 'e'), one of the host of brandy/sherry producers whose names and products are in evidence all over the country.

*Fundador, probably the most widely known Spanish brandy, was first produced in 1874. It has 25% pot-still brandy and a fruity, soft roundness from its solera-ageing which makes it very approachable. Fundador accounts for half of all Spanish brandy exports.*

The vineyards of Jerez overlie gently rolling mounds of dazzling white albariza soil, looking like endless hectares of bleached corduroy cloth, and the region itself is surrounded by three distinctive types of terrain.

On one side, the marshes lay out scruffy drainage channels on the land like the grey fingers of a corpse; on another, the mountains of the Cordillera Bética are much more attractive; and, completing the triangle, on the remaining side the Cádiz plains stretch away into a blue haze from the base of the 70-metre (230-ft) drop from the Jerez plateau.

The vineyards are scattered with farmhouses, some chic, some a little threadbare, usually amid clumps of shady trees. Many of the grander residences were originally built for the royal mistresses. The towns are elegant and arresting, with an abundance of carved wood and stone features, and widespread use of deep-colour glazed tiling and pottery. In tactile terms, it is a very satisfying environment where stone, wood, wrought iron and leather have not yet been wholly supplanted by brick, extruded plastics and other assorted synthetics. The hotels are a joy.

## History

Brandy and sherry have developed cheek by jowl with each other, the latter's fortification with grape spirit being an integral part of its formation and character. The Moors had been and gone by 1492, leaving the knowledge of distillation as only a part of their legacy, but it was not until 1580 that documents first indicate dealings in *aqua vitae* in the Jerez area. A Jesuit school was built on the proceeds of the sales, so there must have been considerable turnover to finance such a project.

Trade with northern Europe was well established by the 1700s and the style of lower-strength distillate prepared especially for Dutch merchants acquired the name Holandas by which it is still known today. Spain's bodega-owners came to realize the influences of the wooden barrels on the spirit when they started stockpiling it in order to meet orders as they came in. It was then a short step to their incorporating ageing periods as a finishing stage for the distillate.

Spanish brandy came to be accepted as a *bona fide* national product in the 1870s, and even went straight into an export mini-boom when cognac failed due to phylloxera, before succumbing itself to vineyard-infestation. It was during this growth period that the first Spanish brandy brand, Fundador, was founded (by Domecq) and such is its wide distribution today that it is still the first Spanish brandy that many people try.

### Vineyard zones

The brandies of Jerez used to be distilled from vines grown in the area but today priority is given to sherry production, and now less costly wines made elsewhere in La Mancha and Ciudad Real are used, because the high-strength continuous-still spirits put into most blends do not retain individual grape characteristics. Grape-type and origin are therefore less important.

None of the brand-owning firms owns vineyards in these other districts, but most own stills there, many of them in the town of Tomelloso. The spirit is transported to Jerez for solera-ageing and – most importantly – blending.

### Regulations

The general aim of Spanish producers is to make a brandy that is less austere and more giving than cognac, and a first step towards doing so is in their choice of wine. They like a well-balanced source-wine that does not have the 'lip-stinging' acidity cultivated in the Charentes. The Airén grape used is not local to Jerez, nor has it a pronounced flavour; what its wine does have is the better balance and a higher alcoholic strength which is preferred in Spain.

Natural extracts from almonds, cherries, and other fruit are often added to brandies in macer-

*Fortunately, the Moors maintained Iberian vineyards despite the Koranic ban on alcohol.*

ated form to create nuance. In the proportions that apply, the influence is not unlike Scotch malt whisky's being aged in former sherry casks that impart a heavy sherry character to the final spirit.

'Brandy de Jerez' has just recently had its own official '*denominación de origen*' confirmed, the Spanish equivalent to cognac's *appellation contrôlée*, and all brandy bearing the name must be made according to its regulations.

The Consejo Regulador, the professional body that administers the denomination, monitors all stages of production and ageing and carries out quality control checks.

Jerez brandy is an extension of sherry-production, and not parallel to it, since it may only be produced by firms which are already recognized as sherry-producers.

### Distillation

Jerez distillers have adopted greater freedom in using their stills than the Charentais. They carry out both single and double distillation in their pot-stills, to this day using the old Moorish name, *alquitara*, for both the apparatus and the high-quality spirit they produce, and apply steam or a naked flame to heat them. They also distil to both high and low alcoholic strengths with continuous stills which is very unusual, although some Australian producers do something similar.

These procedures give Jerez producers four types of spirit with which to 'build' a brandy to the specifications they want, but officially they are graded according to alcohol-content. Low-strength spirit distilled to below 70% abv is called holandas and, with its stronger flavours and aromas, is usually the core of a blend of distillates of different strengths. Medium- and high-strength spirits are respectively under and over the 80% abv mark. Some of the other spirits used to go as high as 95% pure alcohol, but new EC regulations have set a ceiling of 86% abv for grape spirits.

## Maturation

The new brandies have any required fruit 'improvers' added before they begin their ageing in oak. The casks have held sherry before, which adds further flavouring elements to the spirit and also takes the tannic edge off the wood.

The 'solera' system of ageing is better known as a part of sherry production, but early testing showed that it was equally effective for brandy. The technique utilizes a convenient minor miracle whereby a small amount of young spirit, when added to a larger amount of more mature spirit, will readily take on the latter's characteristics.

This has the commendable merit of accelerating the maturation process, and the Jerezanos use a kind of 'cascade' transfer routine to keep the 'age-steps' small. Casks are stacked typically four-high in the bodega, and when brandy is drawn off the bottom (and oldest) level prior to bottling, the cask receives the equivalent amount from the next oldest immediately above.

Each level is thus replenished from above, and the youngest (top) level receives newly-distilled spirit. Soleras can, in fact, have up to 30 intermediate stages – called scales, or *criaderas* in Spanish – and these need not be alongside each other; they could even be in different bodegas.

The spirit is moved from one criadera to another – the operation is called 'running the scales' – three or four times a year as sales volume of the brandy requires. Several soleras containing spirit of a single source and age may also run in parallel with each other to achieve reasonable bottling volume when the spirit is drawn off the soleras and combined. The quantity of spirit transferred from each cask must never exceed a third of its volume.

## Label information

Three qualities of Jerez brandy are designated by the Consejo:

**Solera Brandy de Jerez**: This is aged for only six months and predictably indicates the cheaper, high-volume brandy. Sales are falling off now, however, as consumers turn to better-quality styles.

**Reserva Brandy de Jerez**: This deeper-hued amber brandy has to be minimum one year old, and has a slight caramel edge to its flavour with some sweetness too. It also has a more extended aftertaste than the younger category.

*Continuous stills at a Domecq facility. Wine from Airén, Cayetana and Jaén grapes is distilled into Holandas in both pot- and continuous-stills.*

**Solera Gran Reserva Brandy de Jerez**: A much more distinguished brandy, aged for minimum three years, deep mahogany in colour with a toasted, caramel nose. It is round and smooth with a very long finish.

The content of congenerics – the flavouring elements in the distillates – must also be measurably higher in the better-quality brandies. Bottle-strength is usually at about 38% abv, although in fact anything between 34% and 45% abv is actually permitted.

If these minimum ages seem modest besides those that prevail in Cognac and elsewhere, remember that the solera ageing system accelerates the maturation processes they go through.

Jerez producers emphasize the 'dynamic ageing' endowed by soleras compared with the 'static ageing' in the Charentes and other locations.

This makes each Jerez year of ageing worth considerably more than its equivalent elsewhere. A two-year-old pot-still alquitara brandy solera-aged in Jerez can be the equivalent of a four-year-old cognac with its static ageing process.

Spain has sailed close to the wind in the past regarding the packaging and presenting of products so that they look like leading brands.

Laws are tighter now, and the Denominación document for Jerez brandy specifically prohibits 'similarities in phonetics or graphics [which] may give rise to confusion' in the labelling of brandies which are not entitled to use the Jerez denomination.

It is important not to misinterpret labels stating the year in which soleras were established. A date like 1850 is not a vintage year but the date that this particular solera was begun – 'Solera 100 Años' does not mean a 100-year-old solera brandy, but a 100-year-old solera through which the brandy has more recently passed.

*Torres supplied wine to the Spanish American colonies.*

## Places to visit

The whole Jerez area is redolent of centuries of history – a string of invaders over 1500 years, and then 500 years of the Moors; the scores of reckless years when expeditions set off headlong to explore successive coasts of the Americas; the growth of sherry wine and the peaceful invasion of the British to take a hand in it; and the development of brandy-making. Take your pick and follow the paths that interest you.

Within the city itself are a number of churches with important architectural and religious features, and the Casa Domecq is one of several beautiful seigneurial residences that may be visited. Others are the Marquis of Bertemati's Palace, the Perez Luna Palace and the house of the Ponce de Leon family. The old Moorish walled fortress of the Alcazar lies close by the González Byass bodegas.

The city of Jerez is the centre of a far-flung area where grapes for sherry-production are grown and where, in turn, Jerez brandy is distilled. The full name of the city is 'de la Frontera', and a glance at the map reveals a succession of similarly constructed names – Vejer de la Frontera, Chiclana de la Frontera, Arcos de la Frontera. They lie in a line that formerly constituted the boundary between Christian and Moorish territory.

Vejer is one of the famous and very attractive 'white towns' of Andalucía, adventurously positioned atop a crag with a considerable stork population. The view down the Barbate Valley must be the best from a town car park in the whole of Europe, and the corniche approach-road is exciting.

Chiclana, an attractive Andalucían fishing village, has extensive beaches.

Arcos is spectacular from a distance, it too being crouched on a rock outcrop. These towns were built for security but shortage of space did not prevent the people here from having two churches inside the castle walls. Park the car carefully in the main square – one side is a sheer drop to the Guadalete River below.

Palos is another frontier town further north in a separate wine-production zone called Huelva. It is from here that Columbus sailed in 1492 to 'discover' America and Cortés left in 1523 for Mexico. All around is a fascinating landscape of rivermouth sandbars, salt marshes, sand-dunes and beaches sewn with pine and eucalyptus clumps. The extraordinary Donaña National Park protects numerous near-extinct creatures like the

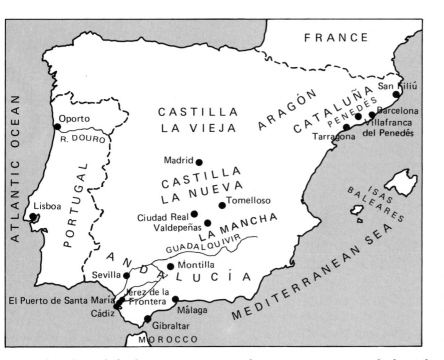

*The Jerez region in the south and Cataluña in the north-east are the only officially designated brandy-production zones in Spain.*

imperial eagle and the lynx; visitors are welcome but you must arrange details in advance.

Horses, wine and bulls fill the consciousness of the Jerezanos and there are frequent fairs that follow these themes.

It was in Cádiz that flamenco singing and dancing began to evolve their forms. Take any opportunity you get to see a good troupe – that is, one that commands quite high ticket prices; you will be impressed at the range of vocal colour and musical texture that is used, and there is a surprising vein of humour that often shows itself.

Inland is Seville, Spain's fourth largest city and the capital of Andalucía. It is a bustling city with plenty for tourists to see in the fields of architecture, fine arts, religious festivals, museums, gardens, elegant shops and restaurants. Nearby is the excavated Roman town of Italica, birthplace of emperors Hadrian and Trajan, with a town theatre that is still being excavated by archaeologists.

Ronda is a marvel, a sierra town cut in two by the most famous of the Guadalevin Gorges. The single window in the centre of the much-photographed bridge used to be the town gaol, from which no one *ever* escaped using knotted-together sheets. Ronda was the cradle of bull-fighting and its 1785 bullring is one of Spain's oldest. The old quarter is pre-15th century Moorish with picturesque streets, and the collegiate church's belfry is a converted minaret.

The sierra roads around the town are austerely

majestic and the Pileta Caves have prehistoric wall-paintings which predate those of Altamira. The caves are believed to have been occupied over 25 000 years ago and the pottery remains found there are the oldest-known specimens in Europe.

*Independencia, a gran reserva, is one of the range of five Osborne brandies. The company was founded by an Englishman called Tom Osborne.*

## LISTINGS

### Blásquez (Hijos de Augustín)

Producers of Felipe II, which is popular in the United States and South America. Anticuario is their middle-range brand and their top-of-the-range is Toison d'Or, a Gran Reserva, shows well in Germany and Italy. The company is part of the Domecq group.

### Labels

Filipe II; Anticuario; Toison d'Or; Gran Reserva

### Bobadilla

The two '103' brands are differentiated by label colour. Etiqueta Blanca (white) is their starter and Etiqueta Negra (black) is a Reserva quality. Gran Capitán is also in the same category but is a little older, finer and is of limited production. All of the brandies are aged in casks that have been used for maturing sherry, giving that distinctive, generous edge to the flavours and aromas. Sales of brandy are about a million cases a year, but the company is also a large producer of casks in Spanish and American oak (although the former are becoming scarcer as the home forests thin out).

### Labels

Etiqueta Blanca; Etiqueta Negra; Gran Capitán

### BOBADILLA 103 ETIQUETA NEGRA

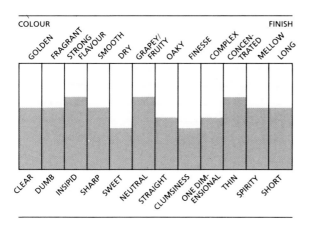

### Bodegas Internacionales

Gran Duque d'Alba is an important de luxe brand in the Spanish domestic market, ranking third in that sector, but it is also one of the internationally-recognized Spanish brandy names. Production of the Gran Reserva brandy is being increased from its present annual 50 000 cases so it should be having a more prominent showing in export markets in the coming years. An entire bodega – Bertemati – is devoted to the brand. It has 4 000 casks and five levels – scales – including the solera itself, from which the fully-matured brandy is drawn to go on sale. The company markets a number of other brandies of varying importance under the brand names of subsidiary firms, but Primado, another Gran Reserva, is the only one with any appreciable distribution.

### Labels

Gran Duque d'Alba; Gran Reserva; Primado

### GRAN DUQUE D'ALBA

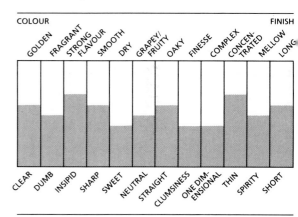

*Fundador – a fruity, soft, round brandy.*

## Caballero, Luís

Milenario – a Gran Reserva – is the main brandy produced by a firm first established in 1830, but occupying bodegas that date from the 1600s. The other two are Chevalier and Derano, but these are not widely distributed.

Production is limited anyway, the company's brandy efforts going into the orange-flavoured ponche (punch) they produce. Caballero has its own vineyards and is based in Puerto Santa María, where the company owns the picturesque Moorish castle of San Marcos.

The Cabeleiros [*sic*] were originally from Galicia in the north-west of Spain, from where they did well supplying Jerez brandy-producers with timber to make casks. When they opened a warehouse in Jerez, they decided to go one step further and put the brandy in the casks themselves. The first Luís Caballero was an imaginative salesman and when the liner *Infanta Isabel de Borbón* made its maiden voyage to Argentina in 1925, he went with it and took along over 3000 cases of Caballero brandy.

Milenario is from a solera that was established in 1795 and the brandy is available in a traditional bottle or an attractive decanter.

## Domecq

Fundador ('Founder') is aptly named since it was the first-ever Spanish brandy brand and is still usually the first experience most people have in tasting brandy from that country. The story goes that a Holandas shipment from Domecq to Amsterdam was sent back because it was late. The brandy was left for over five years in casks that had previously contained sherry until staff tasted it and drew the attention of Pedro Domecq to the changes in it that had taken place. He was most impressed.

That moment was said to be the impetus towards the establishing in 1874 of both the brand and the blend of Fundador brandy. It has 25% pot-still brandy and a fruity, soft roundness from its solera-ageing that makes it very approachable. While its sales have dropped in Spain to 5% of the market – Spaniards have been energetically trading up in recent times – its popularity abroad is undiminished. Half of all Spanish brandy exports are of Fundador.

Tres Cepas is also a Solera brandy, but is the Domecq starter below Fundador in the range. Carlos III is the number two Reserva Jerez brandy on the Spanish market; it is made from 50% pot-still Holandas and has a drier, smoky finish.

*Colour comparison of four brandies in the Domecq range.*

There is 80% pot-still distillate in Carlos I which is richer and oakier again, while Carlos I Imperial is 100% pot-still produce and 16–18 years old. It is rich, oaky and dry but fruity, a lot of substance to 'chew' on. Carlos I Imperial comes in a decanter-style bottle and is top of the Domecq range, replacing Marqués de Domecq which has now been withdrawn.

Domecq has three distilleries in different parts of Spain where wine from Airén, Cayetana and Jaén grapes is distilled into Holandas in both pot- and continuous stills, both types made of copper. The old Cognac tradition of heating the pot-stills by a naked flame is retained, here by use of log fires. The first distillation is called the *flema* (Cognac's *brouillis*) and reaches 30–35% abv and the second reaches 65–70% abv. Some press wine from sherry grapes is also distilled. Different spirits are aged in ex-oloroso sherry casks and then advance to separate soleras from which different brand-styles will eventually emerge.

By rights the Domecq dynasty should have been distilling armagnac over the past 200 years because the family's roots are in Gascony.

### Labels

Carlos I; Carlos I Imperial; Carlos III; Fundador; Marqués de Domecq; Tres Cepas.

### DOMECQ FUNDADOR

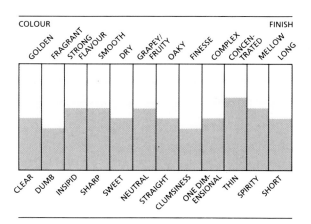

*Domecq has three distilleries, located in different parts of Spain, and uses continuous- as well as pot-stills (as here).*

## DOMECQ CARLOS I

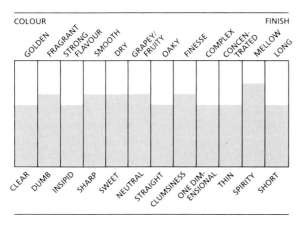

### Garvey

The company has been achieving a higher profile in target export markets with its top-end 20-year-old Gran Reserva Renacimiento in its elegant decanter, and Reserva Gran Garvey. Standard Esplendido has about a tenth of the domestic market. Garvey was established in 1780 by an Irish émigré from County Waterford and is best-known for its San Patricio fino sherry, although sales of the brandies are about a third of a million cases – roughly equal to those of the sherries. Garvey has exported brandy since 1858 and is a warranted supplier to the Spanish royal family.

### Labels

Esplendido; Gran Garvey; Renacimiento

### *González Byass*

There is a range of five brands with three of them – Insuperable, Soberano and Byass 96 – broadly on the same quality level but showing different styles. They are all straight Jerez brandies with just over a year's solera ageing, but Soberano has about a quarter of the 'standard' solera sales. Conde Duque is a Gran Reserva with minimum three years in the solera and the flagship brand, Lepanto, is 15 years old. It was the top-selling de luxe Spanish brandy until it was recently ousted by Cardenal Mendoza. Lepanto is made from 100% Holandas spirit, which is pot-distilled and aged in old American oak casks that have previously been used for maturing sherry.

Manuel María González began producing sherry and brandy in 1835 in bodegas that were already very old. After a few years he brought an English wine-merchant, called Robert Byass, into the business to help increase distribution. Today Soberano is one of the world's second-largest selling brandies, with 25 million bottles a year, and Tío Pepe is the world's top-selling sherry fino. The company owns 1800 hectares of vineyards and it was the first to set up a modern viticultural laboratory in the sherry district, establishing scientific quality-control methods and clonal selection of vines. The company is still family-owned.

Visitors are welcome on weekdays, but please telephone ahead. The bodegas are beside the Alcázar and cathedral in Jerez. The circular bodega layout is remarkable, making it look like a miniature Astrodome; it was designed by Gustave Eiffel of Paris tower fame. It is highly original, as was the company's approach to harvesting, for which they designed special boxes to prevent grapes fermenting before they were delivered to the winery.

González Byass recently launched their own cognac, an XO quality from vines in the Charentes that they have owned since 1929.

### Labels

Byass 96; Conde Duque; Insuperable; Lepanto; Soberano.

## GONZÁLEZ BYASS SOBERANO

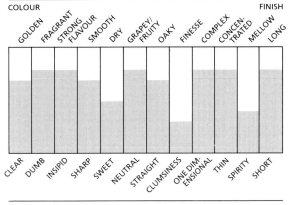

## GONZÁLEZ BYASS INSUPERABLE

## GONZÁLEZ BYASS BYASS 96

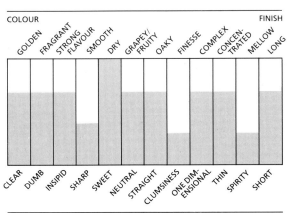

## GONZÁLEZ BYASS CONDE DUQUE

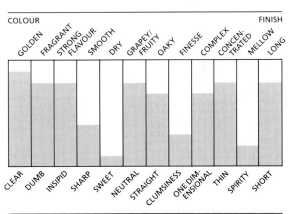

## GONZÁLEZ BYASS LEPANTO

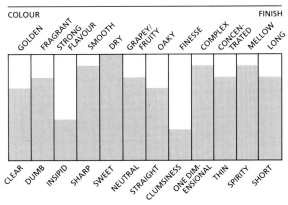

*Soberano, the second-largest selling Spanish brandy.*

## Luque, M. Gil

Four carefully-graded brands that figure in each of the three Jerez age categories, plus a 'special'. Memorable is in the Solera group, having aged six months minimum, and Leyenda is a one-year-old Reserva. Waterloo 1815 is a Gran Reserva at minimum three-years-old and Cien Lustros goes much longer – at least 21 years – before release. The latter sells under the Sánchez de Alva label. The style is firm but aromatic and very rounded with appropriate spirit support and a pleasing complexity.

### Labels

Cien Lustros; Leyenda; Memorable; Waterloo 1815

*Waterloo 1815, a Gran Reserva, minimum 3 years-old.*

## M. GIL LUQUE MEMORABLE

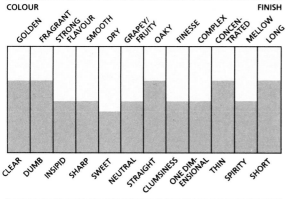

## M. GIL LUQUE LEYENDA

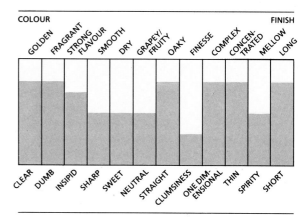

## M. GIL LUQUE WATERLOO 1815

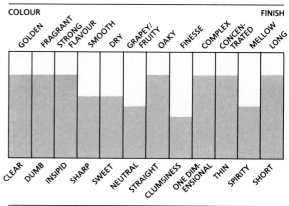

## M. GIL LUQUE CIEN LUSTROS

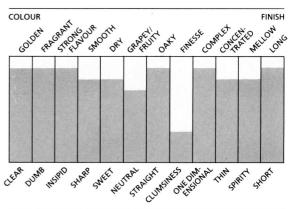

## Núñez, Antonio

Two brands which are of high quality but not widely known. Arrumbador is an above-average 'standard' and Pontifice, in a beautiful decanter, is a Gran Reserva drawn from a large solera resource. Núñez is small, relatively recent in that the company was not formed until 1927, and is a family business, but the brandy stocks are impressive. The little bodega is attractively presented and it is worth telephoning to arrange a visit.

### Labels
Arrumbador; Pontifice

## Osborne

A range of five brandies comes out of these celebrated bodegas. Veterano is the 'standard' and has almost a fifth of its sector's sales. Next up the scale is Magno, which is a Solera Reserva with a range of Holandas spirits to its make-up and at least a year's ageing to give it a more settled persona. It is the top Reserva Jerez brandy in Spain, selling twice as much as the next brand. Independencia, a Gran Reserva, and Carabela Santa María are both on the same quality level but of different styles. Conde de Osborne, in the funny, opaque, tilted bottle designed by Salvador Dalí, is rounded and mellow at over 18-years-old.

Osborne are the biggest brandy-producers in the sherry region with sales of 3¼ million cases a year. There is a specialist brandy complex with 40000 casks in the maturation soleras. The group of four individual bodegas is quite a sight to see on the Puerto-Jerez road. The company was founded in 1772 by an Englishman from Exeter called Tom Osborne, although these days they pronounce the 'e' in the name. The current chairman of the board is Enrique Osborne MacPherson.

### Labels
Carabela Santa María; Conde de Osborne; Independencia; Magno; Veterano

*Osborne, the biggest brandy producer in the Jerez region.*

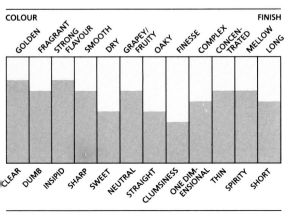

## OSBORNE MAGNO

## OSBORNE CONDE DE OSBORNE

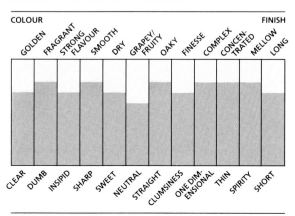

*The Torres family have had vineyards in the Villafranca region of Penedés since the 17th century.*

## Sánchez Romate

Four brands which culminate in one of the very top Spanish brandies. Abolengo is the youngest, followed by El César which is about six years old. Cardenal Cisneros is over ten years old (and sports its own unofficial category of Reserva Especial) and Cardenal Mendoza is *hors d'age* but officially categorized as Gran Reserva. In a short space of time it has become the top de luxe brandy in Spain, displacing González Byass's Lepanto. Cardenal Mendoza was created over a century ago as a genuine family reserve before being launched and named after a famous Spanish soldier who interceded on behalf of Christopher Columbus to obtain royal patronage for his first voyage to America. You can still see the four barrels in which the first brandy was aged.

Cardenal Mendoza is made from low-strength Holandas spirit and then aged for several years in American oak casks that have previously held sherry. The best spirits are then blended and installed in a solera ageing process. Over 17 differently aged brandies go into the blend *before* it is put into the solera system to age further, and it passes through seven successive scales before reaching the final solera stage immediately prior to bottling. It is available in a crystal decanter as well as in its regular, somewhat gaudily-labelled bottle.

There are 15 000 casks in the Mendoza bodega, mainly solera, but including also the static-ageing section.

The firm is old (founded in 1781) and distinguished, having been suppliers to both the Spanish royal family and a past Pope. They also supplied the House of Lords of the British Parliament back in 1909, perhaps confirming the aristocratic character of the brandy; either the House of Commons were not interested in it or they were never offered

*Sánchez Romate, founded in 1781, has been warrant supplier to the Spanish royal family and the Vatican.*

it. The company has five sherry vineyards in addition to well-known bodegas and the firm is still family-owned. For a long time Mendoza was principally an export brand, but recently it has built up its domestic market dramatically.

## Labels

Abolengo; Cardenal Cisneros; Cardenal Mendoza; El César

### SÁNCHEZ ROMATE CARDENAL MENDOZA

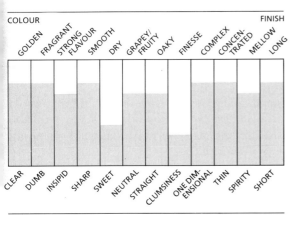

### Sandeman

This is the port and sherry firm that uses the logo of the silhouetted man in the wide-brimmed hat and the black cape, so Capa Negra was a logical choice for the name of the brandy they now market. Although the firm was established by George Sandeman from Perth in Scotland in 1790, it was 1964 before they started producing brandy. Capa Negra is the standard brand and Capa Vieja the de luxe.

### Labels

Capa Negra; Capa Vieja

### Terry, Fernando A. de

Centenario has a fifth of the total sales in the 'standard' Jerez brandy sector. The 1900 brand is a little older and has a proportion of Holandas in its make-up. Imperio is roughly the equivalent of a good VSOP and Primero is big, round and velvety in character. The general style of Terry brandies has the traditional caramelly fullness although it is more muted with the Imperio Gran Reserva. The house-style is partly shaped by the inclusion of fruit infusions in the final blend.

The business was set up in 1883 to include sherry but with some emphasis on brandy. The main brandy bodega is 225 years-old and the long-disused office on a balcony has been left as in a time-warp with its ledgers, desks and paraphernalia undisturbed. The firm is also famous for its Carthusian horses, which were supplied to the Spanish Riding School in Vienna. The stud function is no more but there is a collection of beautiful carriages at their museum which is worth a visit (telephone ahead). Terry is now part of the Harvey group.

### Labels

Centenario; Imperio; 1900; Primero

### TERRY CENTENARIO

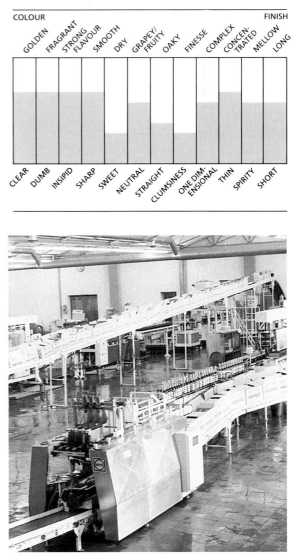

Mechanized bottling at Osborne – over 3¼ million cases of Osborne brandy are sold every year.

79

## Valdespino

Two brands of considerable distinction: Sello Azul (Blue Seal) 1850, a ten-year-old, and Alfonso el Sabio (Alfonso the Wise), which is quite a bit older. The fuller solera-ageing style is punctuated by sherrywood tones which, in blowsier blends, are mistaken for caramel 'padding'. Alfonso the Wise was the king who reconquered Jerez from the Moors.

Valdespino has its own distillery. It is a very old family firm that concentrates obsessively on quality. It is a blender and vineyard-owner, being one of the few Jerez distilleries still making some brandy from Sherry grapes (usually from the third pressing).

The firm has a long lineage, and the family can say they began trading in 1264 when an ancestor was given land by the king after helping expel the Moors from Jerez. They claim to have been distilling since 1500, 50 years before the cognac-makers of France got into their stride, and they have, on show only, the oldest still in the Jerez region. Standing nearly 9m (30ft) high, it is most impressive, although it has not actually produced any spirit for over 100 years.

Valdespino sells about 75 000 cases a year, with Britain, the United States and Holland among its export markets. It also owns the Argueso firm that exports to the United States the cream sherry that has a padlock on the bottle.

There are no organized tours, but a telephone call could result in an informal visit.

### Labels
Alfonso el Sabio; Sello Azul 1850

### VALDESPINO SELLO AZUL 1850

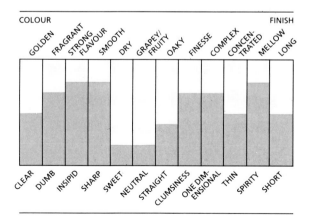

## VALDESPINO ALFONSO EL SABIO

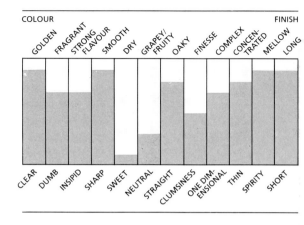

## Williams & Humbert

Small quantities of three brandies fill out the mainly-sherry portfolio of the company formed in 1877 by the marriage of Alexander Williams and Amy Humbert.

Williams is the starter brand, Don Pelayo the Reserva and Brandy Sack, referring to their famous Dry Sack sherry, the Gran Reserva. None of the labels makes specific reference to Jerez so they may well not be entitled to the Jerez denomination.

### Labels
Brandy Sack; Don Pelayo; Williams

*Part of the Osborne range – the opaque tilted bottle was designed by Salvador Dalí.*

# GRAPE BRANDY – PENEDÉS

This location in Cataluña in the north-east of Spain became an officially designated zone for brandy-making in 1985, making it a denomination shared at present by only two companies. Penedés had no tradition of organized commercial brandy-making like Jerez for, although wine-making was long-established there, it was not fortified in style and there was no need for grape-spirit as in Jerez.

However, two wine-producers in close proximity to each other, both established for several generations, started to investigate the possibilities of making good cognac-style brandy in an area already famous for distinguished still and champagne-method sparkling wines.

It was the importance of the commercial and practical success of these two firms that brought about the Spanish denomination of origin for 'Brandy del Penedés' alongside that of Jerez, and the equivalent recognition within the framework of the new European Community's spirits legislation. It was plainly an acknowledgement of what has already been achieved in the zone and demonstrated an expectation of further development to come.

But, for the moment, the story of Penedés is that of these two pioneering producers.

## Mascaró

The Mascaró family have been wine-makers and distillers for three generations now and they created the Mascaró brand in 1945. The brandy is made in the same way as cognac with double-distillation in pot-stills, although Antonio Mascaró Carbonell, the brandy-maker, uses internal steam-heating in the stills instead of a naked flame.

Most of the distilling wines come from Mascaró's vineyards at Villafranca and derive from Spanish vines, the Parellada and the Tempranillo.

The brandies are aged in Limousin oak 'statically', that is to say, at rest in their respective casks cognac-style and not, as in Jerez, by the solera system.

The company makes a range of about a dozen other products, mainly champagne-method sparkling wines and spirits. For what it is worth, they have won gold medals in a number of tasting competitions over the past 20 years. Mascaró is widely regarded as one of the very best brandies in Spain.

There are three brandies, the youngest very slightly sweeter than the others. They are all 40%

*Mascaró's brandies are double distilled in pot-stills.*

abv. The VO Estilo Fine Marivaux is three-years-old and the Narciso Blue Label is five years-old with some spirity depth. The Don Narciso has eight static years but is quite magisterial.

### MASCARÓ NARCISO BLUE LABEL

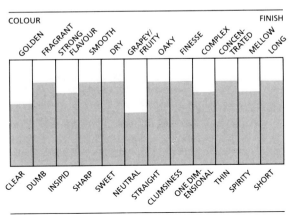

## MASCARÓ DON NARCISO

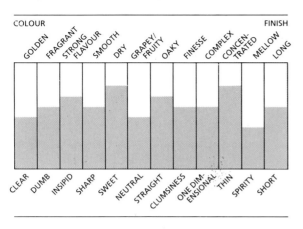

### Torres

The Torres family have had vineyards in the Villafranca area of Penedés since the 17th century. The present business was established in 1870 when one of the family came back to Spain from Cuba and set up in business with his brother to supply wines to the Spanish colonies, principally in Central and South America.

The development of the company over the past 50 years was engineered by Miguel Torres Senior who decided to go for top quality in wine-making, was spectacularly innovative in introducing new vines like Riesling, Gewürztraminer and Muscat to Spain and made the most of new technology in harness with the best traditional production methods.

The Cabernet Sauvignon that he planted evolved into the Gran Coronas wine brand that eventually came to score better marks than Château Latour and other great clarets in a tasting

*Torres Solera Selecta, a full-bodied continuous-still brandy aged in a solera of American oak.*

held in Paris in 1979 – and it was a fifth of Latour's price! There were difficult times, for example during the Civil War when a bomb destroyed a vat and 500000 litres of wine flowed off into the country lanes. However, once the war was over Torres and his wife set off for the United States to open new markets and in New York recently, the Wine Spectator Foundation's critics' survey included Gran Coronas in their list of the world's greatest wines.

Members of the family have areas of special responsibility and Miguel Torres Junior, a gifted oenologist, looks after the entire wine-making and vineyard operation in Spain as well as in Chile. Marimar Torres looks after the 20 hectares (49 acres) of vineyards that the company now owns near Russian River in Sonoma, northern California. In 1986 Chardonnay and Parellada vines were planted, the latter for the first time in the United States, and the first red wines are due now.

*Miguel Torres, double-distilled in copper pot-stills, then aged in French oak for at least 7 years.*

### The brandies

In 1928 the father of Miguel Torres senior began distilling local wines into brandy that was lighter in style to what was then typical in Spain. Although the wines were from Penedés, the method he used for the better brandies was that of Cognac. The main grape was, and today still is, the native Parellada, a high-quality variety that yields light, fresh and fruity wine.

In ascending order, the first two brandies – Torres 5 Solera Selecta and Torres 10 Gran Reserva – are distilled in continuous apparatus and then aged in a solera of American oak. They are quite full-bodied in style and the latter has a marked oakiness of aroma and flavour.

The four other brandies are blends of spirits double-distilled in copper pot-stills and aged 'statically' for different periods in individual French oak casks. Although they show a more airy elegance of style, there is an underlying richness to them all, and a definite 'old gold' rancio to the beautifully decantered Honorable.

Torres' total wine and brandy production is about seven million bottles per year. Visitors welcome – and they arrive in busloads!

## Labels

Torres 5 Solera Selecta; Torres 10 Gran Reserva; Fontenac 5-year-old; Miguel Torres 7-year-old; Miguel I 10-year-old; Honorable 20-year-old.

## TORRES SOLERA SELECTA

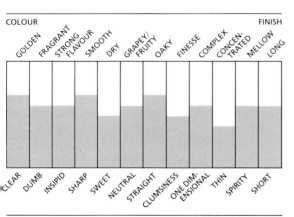

## TORRES 10 GRAN RESERVA

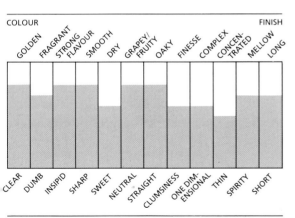

## TORRES FONTENAC

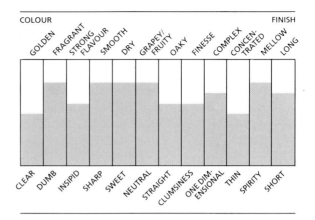

## TORRES MIGUEL TORRES

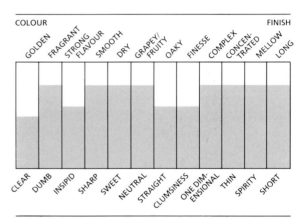

## TORRES MIGUEL I

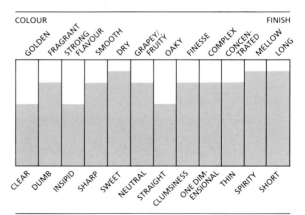

*Fifty years ago, Miguel Torres senior decided to go for top quality in wine-making. His strategy was to make the most of new technology combined with the best traditional production methods.*

## TORRES HONORABLE IMPERIAL

| COLOUR | | | | | | | | | | | FINISH |
|---|---|---|---|---|---|---|---|---|---|---|---|
| GOLDEN | FRAGRANT | STRONG FLAVOUR | SMOOTH | DRY | GRAPEY/FRUITY | OAKY | FINESSE | COMPLEX | CONCENTRATED | MELLOW | LONG |
| CLEAR | DUMB | INSIPID | SHARP | SWEET | NEUTRAL | STRAIGHT | CLUMSINESS | ONE DIMENSIONAL | THIN | SPIRITY | SHORT |

## SPANISH BRANDY

At present, Jerez and Penedés are the only two brandy designations in Spain recognized officially for the purposes of European Community administration. There are, however, further outposts of brandy-production in Spain that have roughly the same status as 'French Brandy', but most of them have purely local or curio value. Brandy is made in Rioja (see below) and elsewhere, but perhaps the highest 'also-ran' profile is that of Montilla-Moriles, a sherry-like wine also produced in Andalucía, and which has almost exactly the same trade structure as that relating to Jerez wine and brandy.

The term 'amontillado' means 'in the style of Montilla', but, ironically, it is now exclusive to sherry and Montilla wines are no longer permitted to use it. Like their Jerez neighbours, the wine-makers of Montilla produce brandy although fewer of their wines are fortified.

## Alvear

There are three brandies in the range of this Montilla producer. Secular is the starter quality, with Senador taking up the middle ground. Top-of-the-range Presidente is regarded as Montilla's finest.

This is the best-known and oldest Montilla-producer and brandy-distiller, the company having been established in 1729 by a local nobleman, in whose family the business remains. The better brandies in the range are made wholly from Holandas and, as with their Jerez counterparts, the wines derive from La Mancha. The brandy was launched in the early part of this century. It is aged through a system of solera and criaderas. Presidente sells in export markets as Conde de la Cortina.

### Labels

Secular; Senador; Presidente

## ALVEAR PRESIDENTE

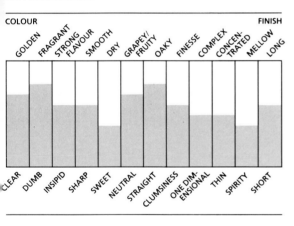

## ALVEAR SECULAR

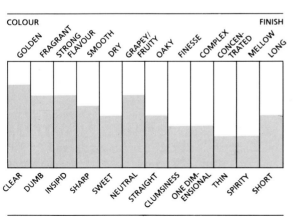

## Bodegas Bilbainas

Rioja has become a popular wine in the past 10 years. However, unlike local producers in other regions, Riojan wine firms have shown little interest in brandy production. One exception is the distinguished firm of Bodegas Bilbainas.

### Label

Imperator

### BODEGAS BILBAINAS IMPERATOR

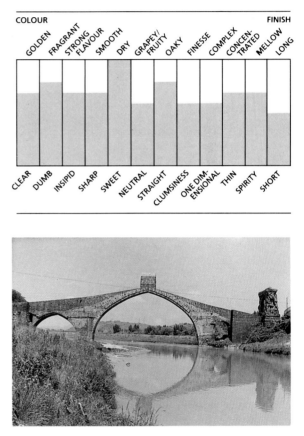

*A bridge landmark near the Torres complex – visitors are most welcome.*

# POMACE BRANDY

Spain also has a pomace brandy, properly called 'aguardiente de orujo', but usually shortened to just orujo. It is made essentially the same way as Italian grappa and French marc and, indeed, one of the well-known producers – Mascaró – prefers to describe its spirit as marc.

While some of the orujos achieve worthwhile local distribution in Spain, they do not have the kind of following that grappa has in Italy. Very little is exported, even less outside Europe.

*An Osborne label designed by Salvador Dalí.*

## Cavas Hill

The company was founded in 1660 by an English immigrant called Hill who planted vines at the El Maset farm he acquired by the tiny village of Moja in Penedés. For a medium-sized firm, it produces today a wide range of limited-production still and sparkling wines, several of them champagne-method. The marc is distilled in copper pot-stills from pomace from Parellada grapes, used in several of the wine-blends.

### Label
Cavas Hill Marc

### CAVAS HILL MARC

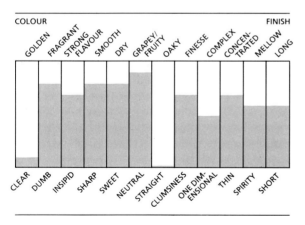

## Larios

This large and successful spirits house, famous for its gin bottle's copy-cat label of Gordon's yellow export livery, does a tasty orujo in two qualities from Málaga pomace.

## Mascaró

The Penedés distiller is better-known for his grape brandies (q.v.), but produces a fine marc that is double-distilled from Xarel-lo Macabeo and Parellada grapes and aged in oak for 5–10 years.

### Label
Mascaró Marc

*Mascaró's marc is double distilled and aged in oak for 5–10 years.*

### MASCARÓ MARC

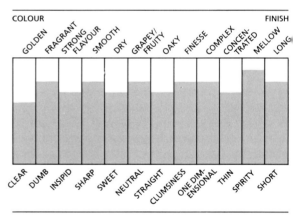

## Places to visit

Cataluña is bounded to the east by the Mediterranean and to the north by the Pyrenees. The coastal resorts of the Costa Brava were among the first in Spain to be developed for package holidays for other Europeans, but there is more to that shoreline than ersatz English pubs and plastic maracas. Ampurias is a vast and fascinating Greco-Roman ruined city complex near L'Escala, and the botanical gardens at Cabo Roig hang spectacularly on a cliff-edge. The corniche road

*A section of the group of four Osborne bodegas on the Puerto-Jerez road, a specialist brandy complex with 40,000 casks in the maturation solera.*

from Begur to Blanes off which they lie is splendid, the best stretch being between San Feliú and Tossa de Mar.

Cataluña has shown national individualism since the ninth century when the wonderfully-named leader, Wilfrid the Shaggy, seceded from Charlemagne's empire; today the province is an autonomous region with Catalan as its official language. It is a rich, expressive tongue, closely related to France's Langue d'Oc, and has a diverse literature.

Cellist Pablo Casals was Catalan, as were Joan Miró and Salvador Dalí, and the vigorous arts environment of Barcelona did much to shape the work of Picasso, who, though born in Málaga, was a student there. Exuberant architecture is to be seen in all directions when you walk about the city, from the ravishing Gothic quarter to the melting-cheese apartment blocks of Gaudí.

The Poble Espanyol by Montjuic in Barcelona is a pretty 'village' made up of famous buildings from all over Spain recreated in reduced scale. Craft shops and restaurants are the main functions of the buildings, which are laid out in streets, squares and alleys. There is plenty of space to wander in, but not so much that one gets tired.

Museums, churches, theatres, an important zoo, galleries – Barcelona really has everything, and is the setting for the 1992 Olympic Games. For something different in sport, seek out a pelota fronton. This is the Basque ball-game played against an end-wall with enormous curved baskets strapped on to the player's arms. The fans place bets without leaving their seats by throwing a trepanned tennis ball with the money in it to the bookmaker standing in the aisle. The sport will be recognized by American visitors from Florida, where there are quite a few frontons (courts).

The serrated peaks of the Montserrat Massif were the setting of Wagner's opera *Parsifal*, and they are also a dramatic location for a Marian shrine that attracts thousands of pilgrims each year. The monastery dates from the ninth century and is surrounded by hermitages with extraordinary panoramic views across the surrounding terrain. The monastery's *Escolanía*, a boys' choir established in the 13th century, sings daily.

Another monastery at Poblet, near Tarragona, sits within an extraordinary perimeter of three defensive walls. The cloister's enormous 30-tap washbasin is Cistercian in style, and the scrollwork on the capitals is outstanding.

Tarragona itself is another multi-layer open-air museum. Dating from perhaps 1000 years BC, there is a Roman city, an early Christian necropolis and a medieval city to visit. Outside the town you can see the Roman aqueduct at Las Ferreres and a fine mausoleum at Centcelles.

# ITALY

Italy has been something of a free spirit in her approach to eaux-de-vie, as also with wine, and because legislation regulating the production of brandy was updated later than in most countries, she has not really received due credit from trade or consumers for what was eventually achieved.

Italian regulations covering brandy production are so strict that they verge on the pharmaceutical and, although today's laws are relatively recent, two centuries ago preunification monarchs were quite far ahead of their time in regulating to protect public health (as well as raise revenue) without banning the drinks altogether.

Until the 1860s, Italy was an aggregation of city-states and wine/brandy traditions were many and varied, helping to create the situation today where there are two national brandy types: grape brandy throughout most of the country and pomace brandy, called grappa, in its northern quarter.

Italy is the world's largest producer of wine and Italians feel their ties to the land very strongly. Even the most city-entrenched, uncalloused executives will retain a weekend link with the family vine-plot in the country and the chances are that the grandfather of the family makes breathtaking artisanal grappa round the back of the house.

## GRAPE BRANDY

If Leonardo da Vinci could produce sketches of helicopters and submarines hundreds of years ahead of his time, he was bound also to have opinions on a simple and contemporary subject such as distillation. Sure enough, he designed several different alembics in the latter part of the 15th century, and even created a number of elixirs.

From the year 1500 onwards, Italian scientists documented distillation researches, and in 1583 the Duke of Savoy granted a distiller the exclusive right to produce brandy on his estates. The brandy was already being double-distilled and was thus expensive, but Jesuits in the region dispensed the spirit as medicine to the poor, thus earning themselves the name of the 'Brandy Fathers'.

*Italy, the world's largest wine producer, turns over about 7 million cases of brandy and grappa a year.*

In the south of the country, the church also played a part when excessive taxation caused the industry there to collapse; friars, especially Dominicans, were among the most enterprising of the smugglers who made sure that supplies continued to be made available.

## History

In 1734, a later Duke of Savoy set up a regulation code for distilleries and under it the industry grew and flourished. In Naples, by the 1750s, three qualities of brandy could be had: standard, refined and 'dephlegmated', which meant that it had been separated from distillation impurities. In 1771 the House of Savoy awarded the first warrant to supply a royal house to a distiller in Nizza Marittima.

The Italian brandy industry has had its share of incomers who helped to shape it. In 1773 a Liverpool merchant, John Woodhouse, landed in Sicily and set in motion the events that would guarantee the importance of Marsala wine. Not long afterwards, Benjamin Ingham established a distillery there to make the brandy necessary to fortify the wine, and in 1812 his nephew, Joseph Whitaker, joined as a partner. Their 'Cognac Vièrge' sold in two qualities and was very popular.

Jean Bouton, from a Charentais family, settled in Bologna in 1820 and set up a distillery. He italianized his name to Giovanni Buton and today the firm is one of the country's top two brandy-makers. The Landy brothers also arrived from France and in 1870 set up an operation to make 'cognac' in Italy.

Brandy was already very popular by the middle of the 19th century and many of the important Italian production companies were formed at this time. Even Paganini, the composer, had plans to establish a distillery on his estate at Gaione, although nothing seems to have come of this idea.

Like every other brandy-producing country, Italy formerly used the word 'cognac' to designate better quality brandy. Indeed, since the winegrowers in the south of France had long made and marketed their own 'Chianti', Italian use of the French term for the leading *eau-de-vie* was regarded merely as an aspect of trade interchange.

In the 1880s, when disease had destroyed the Charentais vineyards, the Cognaçais continued to produce 'cognac' with wine they brought in from Veneto and Campania in Italy, made from the Trebbiano grape. Lionello Stock, founder of one of Italy's most important firms, is said to have remarked as he watched wine-laden ships leaving

*Lionello Stock founded his company in Trieste in 1884.*

Trieste for Bordeaux one day, 'So we too, here in Trieste, can make cognac.' It was but a short step to the Italians themselves producing the brandy and calling it 'cognac'.

Apart from the question of geographic origin, this was not an outrageous idea since Ugni Blanc, the vine adopted in Cognac after the phylloxera disaster, is the same vine as the Trebbiano used in Italy for making brandy wine.

Nevertheless, in 1948 the Italians signed an agreement not to use 'cognac' on their labels, and in 1956 the Italian Brandy Institute was formed to regulate, foster and monitor production of the spirit, now officially rechristened 'brandy'. This did not cause much dissent since there was a widespread feeling in Italy that Italians had invented the word 'brandy'. In the old Piedmontese language, *branda* was the translation for aqua vitae.

The regulations also acknowledged a more lyrical word – '*arzente*' – culled by the celebrated poet d'Annunzio from a medieval term used by friars at Monticchio for a brandy they produced. In 1930, Ramazzotti adopted arzente for one of their brands, which helped get the word on to the statute book when the law was formulated.

## The brandy

Italian brandy is light in taste and smooth in texture and finish, although the flavours and aromas are positive and well-balanced. What characterizes the approach to producing brands is a high median quality level across the board without the fringe extremes of raw young brandies or exalted, very old ones. It is a mainly two-tier market of standard and de luxe brandy, rather like the world Scotch whisky market was until single malts moved in and broke up the traditional rigidity.

Brandy and grappa together turn over about seven million cases, fairly evenly divided, but both sectors are in a state of flux at the present time. Grape brandy in Italy has been in gently accelerating decline during the tail-end of the 1980s, due not so much to discontent with brandy itself as to a move by consumers away from 'brown spirits'. At least one company has recently stopped making brandy. Less volume is being drunk in favour of better quality. Two firms, Stock and Buton, continue to dominate sales with about 60% of the home market and much of the export effort.

## Production zones

Italians are different in their approach to brandy production in that they allow the wine-making and distillation functions to operate completely separately. They have a comprehensive appellation system for their wines (*Denominazione di Origine Controllata*) that is based, as in other countries, on the typicality of production from a given area, but for brandy they have moved away from the idea of geographic unity.

The types of wines favoured for distillation are made in Veneto, Emilia Romagna, Trentino, Alto Adige and Sicily in the south. These are areas of hot summers and cold winters with soils that hold a lot of lime. The grape variety is less important than that the vines be wholesome and disease-free because the continuous stills used to produce most Italian brandy take individuality out of the spirit while retaining broad grapey flavours and aromas.

The wines are then transported to big cities like Milan, Turin and Bologna where the brandy is distilled and aged in totally unromantic, hangar-like buildings in the suburbs, far removed from the sunny slopes in the country where the grapes are grown. This does not mean, however, that the quality or character of Italian brandy is diminished in any way. Indeed, the Italians reason that quality need not be tied in with designated geographic origin because the most important aspects are careful viticulture and viniculture, wherever the grapes are grown, and the correct distilling, maturation and blending skills.

Little, if any, Italian brandy is lovingly hand-crafted in picturesque, ivy-covered stillrooms – that is all left to the grappa-makers. Consequently, there are no special items like vintaged, or very old, or single-property brandies.

The well-known brand-owning firms are essentially blending, bottling and marketing organizations like a large part of the trade in Cognac. Indeed, the broad structure of the trade is similar to that in Charentes. Considerable capital is needed to finance stocks that might have to mature for anything up to a dozen years or more.

*Buton's Vecchia Romagna range is produced from Ugni Blanc grapes – much of it is matured in oak casks.*

## Distillation

Continuous stills are used to make most Italian brandies and the still strength must not exceed 86% abv. This gives the spirits a lightness, without losing the fruit characteristics of the grapes, but pot-still spirit production gives the blender more options in creating a specific house-style, rather as the Spanish do with their Holandas. Another option used in Italy is to distil certain spirits three times – very unusual, and expensive, but it does take place.

*Few countries can offer the range of historic, traditional and cultural attractions found in Italy.*

## Maturation

The minimum legal ageing period is one or two years in oak casks, depending on ultimate destination, although many brands age for considerably longer. There are tax benefits for companies who age their brandies for longer, and many of them take advantage of the scheme.

The type of oak to be used for ageing is not specified by law, but most comes from Angoulême or the Limousin in France, or Slavonia in Yugoslavia.

## Label information

Standard blends are usually aged for about six years and de luxes for about ten. The lighter nature of Italian brandy is such that greatly extended ageing confers no benefits, and ten years is about as old as most brands aspire to.

With this in mind, label terms like Vecchio (Old) or Stravecchio (XO or Extra Old) are, of course, relative. French terms like Vieille Réserve and VSOP also occur but, apart from separating different brands in a single range, are cosmetic. The Italian certification of extra maturation over the minimum enables specific ages to be indicated on labels and they refer to the youngest brandy in the blend.

Sugar and caramel may be added to the degree accepted in brandy-making elsewhere, and 'aroma enhancement' – oak infusions – of up to 3% is permitted.

Minimum bottling strength is 38% abv and most brands are 40% abv, but allowance is made for higher-strength brandies and the upper ceiling is 60% abv.

## Places to visit

There is probably no other country in the world with such an exhilarating array of places to visit and sites to see as Italy, no matter which part your travels take you to.

As indicated above, there are five main grappa-production areas, with a few one-off operations in, for example, Tuscany and Umbria.

Piedmont has the captivating, misty slopes of the famous Barolo vineyards, and just nearby they make sumptuous Asti sparkling (i.e. 'spumante') wine and those 'lifestyle' vermouths. The Anthony Quinn movie *The Secret of Santa Vittoria* was based on Cinzano's cellars, which go deep into a hillside and whose entrances were disguised by walling them off during the Second World War. In this way the near-hollow hill full of bottles of wine was saved from looting when the German army occupied the area.

Alba, Casale Monferrato and Canelli are three grappa-producing towns worth a visit. The Sacra of San Michele is a very old Benedictine monastery in a spectacular site on the lip of a ravine, and its abbey is a marvel in its own right. It may have been a monk from here who designed France's famous Mont St Michel, which post-dates San Michele and is remarkably similar to it in lay-out.

To the north is famous Lake Maggiore, with its manicured villas and the impossibly beautiful Borromean Islands whose aromatic, spectacular gardens even make them smell wonderful. To the south is neighbouring Liguria where, even today, there is no road linking all five villages of the Cinqueterre (the railway goes through the mountains and is perhaps the world's only rural underground system). The coastal vineyards are so steep that workers could only reach them by boat.

Trentino shares the north-eastern corner of Italy with German-speaking Alto-Adige, the South Tyrol. The mountains are spectacular but mostly accessible for touring. Embedded in the Brenta Massif are the Genova Valley, with its granite wildness and the Nardis Waterfall, and Lake Tovel, reached through great gorges, where Alpine brown bears still roam the wooded shores. Go up Monte Paganella by cable-car for panoramas of the Dolomites, the Alps and Lake Garda.

The vast serrations of the Dolomites may be gazed at from close quarters on the extraordinary Dolomite Road that runs from Bolzano to Cortina. From the comfort of a car you can enjoy the sort of views normally accorded only to mountaineers as the road presents you with a succession of lovely

*The wines used in Italian brandy originate in the northern and Sicilian countryside, although the actual distillation is carried out in the larger cities of the north.*

lakes, gorges, peaks, wildlife (if you use your eyes) and pretty villages trowelled into the landscape. Grappa is produced in Rovereto and San Michele.

Friuli is the easternmost part of Italy, where the coastline curves round towards the Yugoslav frontier. Trieste, much fought-over in the past, is the main port on the Adriatic and the base of the giant brandy and grappa producer, Stock, whose premises may be visited. Udine is a pretty town that sits on a hill with a main alleyway encircling it and a fine 16th-century castle at the summit. The Renaissance Piazza della Libertà is regarded as one of Italy's most beautiful squares and there are numerous Gothic features throughout the town.

Aquilèia has Roman ruins and grappa-making may be seen at Gorizia, Percoto and Faedis.

Veneto has perhaps the most famous sights of all; everyone knows of Venice, with its unique city waterways, St Mark's Square and Basilica, the Doge's Palace, the Grand Canal with its Ca' d'Oro

and other palaces, the Scuole, the Ghetto, the Frari Quarter and the main canal, lined with Renaissance villas, on the glass-working island of Murano.

Verona's Roman Arena is glorious as a setting for *Aida* and the Scaligeri's castle, bridge and tombs are supremely atmospheric.

Lake Garda to the west is a beautiful setting for touring, Treviso has an interesting and picturesque Old Town within its 15th-century ramparts and Padua has frescoes by Giotto in the Scrovegni Chapel.

The Berici and Euganeian hills are also good for pleasantly-paced touring and from 1828 m (6000 ft)-high Monte Grappa it's said you can see Trieste on a clear day. Bassano, near by, is a pottery town as well as an important grappa centre. Other Venetian *grappa* locations are Conegliano, Sant'-Ambrogio, Rastignano and Pedemonte.

Lombardy is dominated by Milan, the city of the Viscontis and the Sforzas, where you can walk

*The Stock company grew very quickly and built a number of factories. Their 'brandy cathedral' at Portogruaro features row upon row of double-decker vats.*

among the statues and pinnacles on the roofs of the white marble cathedral as well as within it; wander the galleries with works by da Vinci, Michelangelo and numerous other famous names at every turn; join the 3000 spectators at La Scala opera house.

At Pavia, the Carthusian monastery the Certosa is one of Italy's great buildings, with rich and sustained embellishment of the 15th-century Gothic/Renaissance architecture. The Visconti family founded the monastery in 1396 and continued to finance the vastly ornate work over the following two centuries. Successive generations of them are buried there.

For a modest fee you can take your car round the race-track at Monza, and Bergamo, where the *commedia dell'arte* was born, retains its 16th-century upper city in almost unchanged condition within its protective Venetian ramparts.

Lake Como is the irresistible draw and indeed it is lovely. Como town, with its all-marble cathedral that took 400 years to build, merits some time. Boat trips leave from here, and you can take the hydrofoil if you are in a hurry.

Bellagio has a unique position at the tip of the promontory formed by the lake splitting into two branches. The town is a delight, with narrow streets, beautiful walks, comfortable hotels and restaurants and the gorgeous Serbelloni and Melzi villas to visit.

## LISTINGS

### Branca

A standard, widely-distributed brand – Brandy Branca Stravecchia – with no indication given as to how 'extra old' it is. The Branca di Romanico family were Italian counts who set up a distillery in 1845 in Milan. Their famous Fernet was the mainstay of their initial success, but in 1892 they introduced their 'Vieux Cognac Croix Rouge' which immediately did very well. A further claim to fame was their oak brandy-ageing vat which, at almost 90 000 litres, was, perhaps not surprisingly, the biggest in Europe. Today the company distil and bottle at their own premises in Milan.

### Buton

One of the top two brandy firms in Italy. Their Vecchia Romagna range is partly differentiated by label colours: Etichetta Nera (black) is a three- to five-year-old blend of pot- and continuous still spirits; Etichetta Oro (gold) is a seven-year-old blend and 100% pot-still derived. There used to be a white label (Etichetta Bianca) but it has been displaced by top-of-the-range Riserva Rara which is blended from pot-still brandies of a minimum age of 15 years. It was created to celebrate the company's 170th anniversary in 1990. All the brandies are from Trebbiano (i.e. Ugni Blanc) grapes and maturation is in small oak casks, an approach which imparts greater wood-influence.

The company was set up in 1820 by Frenchman Jean Bouton and an Italian nobleman; today it is owned by descendants of the de'Medicis and the traditions of the past are highly-valued by them. Buton may well be the only large firm left in Italy still using the old-style swan-necks on their copper pot-stills.

Buton has a third of the domestic brandy market and its products are marketed widely in Europe, but overseas distribution is undeveloped. It distils, blends and bottles but owns no vineyards, although many of its grape-growers have been supplying it for several generations.

Visitors are welcome to the 'City of Brandy' in Bologna with a telephone call in advance until the visitors' centre is completed in 1991.

## BUTON VECCHIA ROMAGNA ETICHETTA NERA 3–5 YEARS-OLD

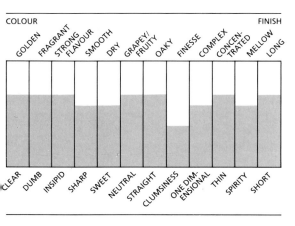

## BUTON ORO 7 YEARS-OLD

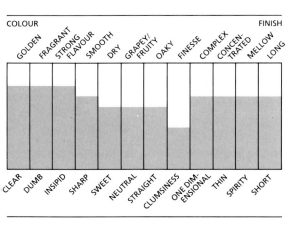

## BUTON RISERVA RARA 15 YEARS-OLD

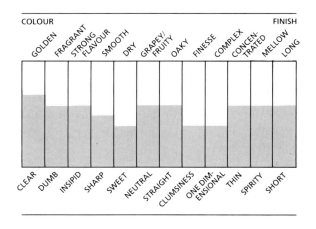

### Camel
Camel has a range of four brandies distilled at Udine in Friuli in north-east Italy, an area that is better-known as a stronghold of grappa. The brand-name is Fogolar (hearth). A master distiller, Giuseppe Tosolini, re-established the firm in 1951 when he inherited it from his in-laws.

The 'normale' is the Brandy Nature which is described on the label as 'invecchiato' (aged); Gran Riserva Bollino Oro confusingly comes in two qualities – three years and six years old; Brandy Riserva dal Fogolar has a rustic label written in dialect and is quite a woody 12-year-old.

### Carpene Malvolti
There are two brandies from this firm, a Stravecchia Riserva and an Antica Annata, both giving indications of long ageing. Unusually for Italy, they are bottled at 43% abv.

The company title is composed of the names of the two original partners: Antonio Carpene, who founded the firm in 1868, and Angelo Malvolti, who joined him not long afterwards. Carpene is regarded as the founder of modern Italian oenology. He did much original research, corresponded with Pasteur and Koch and established the famous viticultural college at Conegliano. He was responsible too for the technical development of sparkling wine and the modern company's brand is one of the best in the world. Carpene was ageing brandy for extended periods as far back as 1871. In those days he produced a 'Cognac Fine Champagne' for 245 lire per hectolitre – and the cask came free.

## Florio

Sadly, this name is included here only to inform that the company no longer produces brandy. It means the conclusion of a colourful and distinguished distilling history and the loss of two important brands, Florio itself and Ingham.

The former had three qualities, including the interesting dry Extrasec, and the latter, four, with its Riserva VSOP at the top end. The company still produces marsala and other wines as part of the Cinzano group.

*Buton brandies are distilled from Trebbiano grapes.*

## Landy Frères

All that seems to be left of a company that was enterprisingly fostered in the past is a simple, uncomplicated French-sounding brandy, Saint Honoré. The brand is now part of the Seagram Italia group. In 1870, the two Landy brothers arrived in Bologna from France with the specific aim of producing 'cognac' there. Everything associated with the enterprise was brought in from France, right down to the labels for the bottles which were printed in Cognac – everything, that is, except the wine that made the brandy. They even registered their Tre Stelle ('Three Stars') brand with the authorities in Cognac in 1911, yet Landy Frères is also thought to be the first Italian firm to use the term 'brandy'.

## Martini & Rossi

In 1840, a small partnership called Martini & Sola bought an established factory at Pessione and went on to do well. When Sola died in 1879, Luigi Rossi succeeded him and Martini & Rossi was formed. The company is known world-wide for its vermouths, but closer to home it is also long-established as a producer of high quality sparkling wine and brandy.

Vecchio Piemonte, a brand long-associated with Martini & Rossi, is produced at Pessione near Turin (where there is also a beautiful wine museum). The Cavallino Rosso brand was acquired with the G. R. Sacco firm and it too is now produced and bottled at Pessione.

## Oro Pilla

This is the well-established large-volume counterpart of the hand-made Villa Zarri brandy (q.v.), the proprietor of which owns both names. Stauroforo Pilla set up the company in Veneto in 1919 in the chaotic aftermath of the First World War. There are four brandies to the Oro Pilla range: a young 'normale', or standard; the black-labelled Scudo Nero, a Riserva of six years' ageing; the gold-labelled Riserva Speciale, a minimum eight-year-old and, unusually for Italy, an elegant 20-year-old Speciale Selezione which also, a little pointlessly, sports a vintage date.

## Ramazzotti

There are two brandies of similar quality but different ages. Both are Riserva; one is a five-year-old, the other a seven-year-old, but it is the younger of the two that has the VSOP tag on the label. They are bottled at 42% abv.

The company was founded in 1815 by an ambitious young member of an old family in Emilia, an ancestor of whom had once been commander of the papal army. Even in the free and easy days of the last century, the company never described its brandy as 'cognac'.

## Seagram Italia

The René Briand brand that now belongs to this multinational firm has retained its French persona with, for example, its trademark a '*marque deposée*' rather than a '*marchio depositato*'. There is a standard and a Vieille Réserve, both of them 40% abv.

The other well-known brand in the Seagram stable here is also pseudo-French, the Landy Frères' (q.v.) Saint Honoré.

## Stock

There is a certain amount of ad hoc adaptation of brands according to destination markets, but basically there are three qualities. The 'normale' is described as '84 VSOP' and three years-old;

Stock 84 Gran Riserva.

straight Stock 84 is a six year-old and the XO is 8–9 years old. The Styles are light with more wood intensity and sweetness showing in the longer ageing.

Stock is one of the two top-selling brands in Italy. They have always had a high profile in their advertising, showing flair and style. Brandy bottles two metres high strolled the pavements of Vienna at the turn of the century—complete with walking stick and spats—and they were among the very first commercial firms anywhere to advertise on radio and television.

Stock's 'brandy cathedral' at Portogruaro shelters row upon row of double-decker vats, all brimful of maturing spirit of up to 20 years of age.

Lionello Stock was Dalmatian by birth and Trieste was part of the Austro-Hungarian Empire when he set up in business there in 1884. The company grew large very rapidly and its policy was to build factories in its export markets. This led to many of its east European plants being confiscated after the last war, but it has bounced back and its products are in about 120 countries today. This presence is partly achieved through distilling arrangements with local firms, as in Australia, where Penfolds make Stock brandy to prescription from Australian grapes.

### STOCK 84

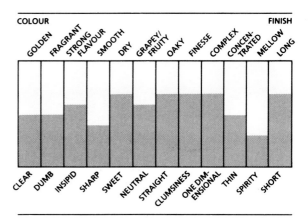

### STOCK 84 VSOP

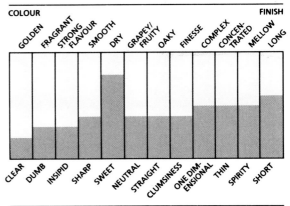

### GOCCIA DI CHARDONNAY

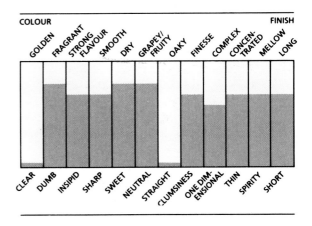

### Labels

Stock 84; Stock 84 VSOP; Goccia di Pinot Chardonnay Stock XO

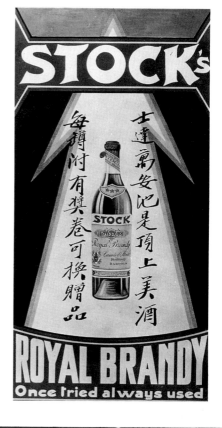

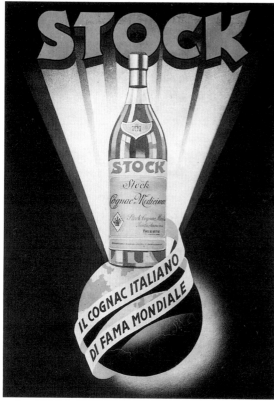

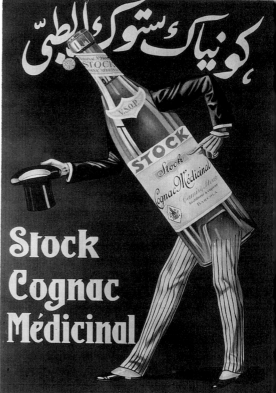

*Stock was a pioneer in product marketing. Its adverts have always been executed with flair, imagination and style.*

## STOCK XO 9 YO

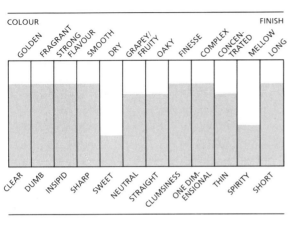

## Villa Zarri

This is Italian brandy-making with all the stops pulled out – a hand-reared, carefully-honed, aristocratic spirit. Leonida Zarri is the proprietor of Oro Pilla (q.v.) but, although the address is the same, the two brandies are separate operations.

## VILLA ZARRI

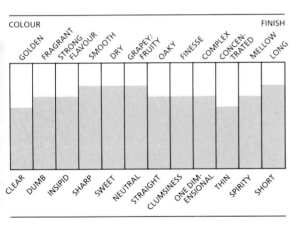

The current Villa Zarri *acquavite* – an upmarket name for brandy – is a vintaged 1986 from Trebbiano (Ugni Blanc) grapes grown in the Chianti zone of the Tuscan hills and in the Romagnoli hills. The wine is double-distilled in Charentais pot-stills to 70% abv and aged for nine months in new Slavonian, Limousin and Tronçais oak before longer passage (about 21 months) through smaller, used Limousin oak casks. During this time it is gradually reduced to 43% abv with distilled water. No boisé or other additive is used.

The centrepiece of the plant at Castelmaggiore is the delightful mustard-and-cream villa in its own little park, beyond which lie the industrial acres of the Pilla maturation sheds. The villa is 16th century, was owned by the noble Angelelli family and has its own little chapel in one of the wings. It is open to the public and regularly holds concerts, ballets and fashion shows.

*Villa Zarri Acquavite – distilled from Trebbiano grapes.*

# GRAPPA

Grappa originated as the poor man's brandy. Who else but poor men would gather the assorted lees of pips, skins and stalks (the pomace) left in the vat after wine has been vinified and drawn off, spray them with water and distil the mixture to extract the weak alcoholic vestiges left in them?

This is essentially how grappa is made and although its production began many generations ago in order to provide country families with a rough, multi-purpose spirit that was at its best keeping out the cold in the formidable Alpine winters, peasant ingenuity for getting the best out of very little enabled it to evolve towards much higher planes.

The best grappa comes from fresh, moist pomace from grapes that have not been too harshly pressed, making better flavours and sugar-content available. It should be distilled immediately after the wine has been drawn off, or within 24 hours at the outside. Beyond that time the material loses the grape flavours and aromas, reducing the quality of the final distillate.

Red grapes yield a quite full-bodied, slightly sweeter spirit that is warming and lends itself to ageing in oak casks, while white grapes produce a more delicate yet aromatic spirit that is better finished in glass or stainless steel to retain its fresh zestiness. Some makers maintain that grappa is a 'living' product and that, like wine and unlike brandy, it matures in bottle, 'becoming harmonious and complete'.

Grappa undoubtedly carries the flavours and aromas of the grapes from which it is distilled, but there is a different focus in what it presents to the drinker. It is like tasting the skin rather than the pulp or juice when you bite into a grape – closely connected but with a changed emphasis.

Pulp flavours are relatively uncomplicated in a grape, but the skins and other parts of the fruit are packed with minute quantities of highly concentrated substances which have the chance to come over in a pomace distillation and endow the flavours that occur in these spirits with great complexity and range.

## History

Grappa is a highland peasants' drink. Its traditional heartlands are in the north of Italy because that is where the country's greatest concentration of mountains is. In this thrifty country economy, anything that could not be eaten straight away had to be preserved and stored. Fruits in every region were fermented and made into rudimentary brandies, and in the mountain wine-producing areas the dominant fruit was, of course, the grape.

Wine and grappa would be produced for the family and any surplus sold. Traditionally, the pomaces from different wine-making operations would be distilled together; the single-variety grappa available today is a recent development.

In the 19th century little mobile stills would be trundled around the villages of northern Italy to distil the farmers' pomace. The distiller was paid with a share of each distillation run, called the *mondure*, and his living came from selling those grappas on.

As Italy's vine register was regulated and drastically reduced in preparation for the new Wine Law that came into operation in 1963, it was only the fact that these mountain wine-producers continued to cultivate traditional local vines that prevented their becoming extinct.

The main production areas are also the sources of several of Italy's most important wines, Piedmont (Barolo and Barbaresco), Trentino (Gewürztraminer), Friuli (Pinot Grigio), Veneto (Valpolicella and Soave) and Lombardy (Valtellina) being the regional locations. Producers make grappas from the pomace of some of these single wines as well as from single grape varieties.

A new idea took hold in the early 1980s – that of distilling whole grapes, less the stalks, to make a kind of 'super-grappa' called Ue. Benito Nonino, who came up with the idea after a trip to Alsace where a lot of fruit brandy is made (see page 17), had to obtain authorization from three different Italian ministeries to produce the new brandy. Now the idea has been taken up by a number of other producers, including one in California.

## The brandy

No one adds caramel to grappa and the flavours and aromas are largely pristine, particular and straight. Those flavours – some would say lack of them – present themselves within very narrow parameters with few of the wide range of fruit and flower cross-references often applied to descriptions of wines and grape brandies.

Intense grapiness and oily roundness will show in good grappa but will be balanced by elegance and structure; those that are aged in wood have an extra dimension. Both styles – aged and unaged – are equally valid. The taste is worth acquiring and, as in armagnac, there is a wide range of style and character, from the almost unpalatably rough and rustic to the ineffably sublime.

Grappa experienced a boom in Italy in the mid-1960s and now it is increasingly catching on in world markets as a high-quality brandy with fast-approaching designer status. It is doing well in the United States and several California distilleries have begun to produce grappas, including one from the Zinfandel grape.

Many of the grappa producers of Italy have the standing of artists in the community and, indeed, their approach to making grappa has many of the attributes of a craftsman in the creation of an artifact – dedication, restless study and adjustment of production techniques, single-mindedness and the desire to handle absolutely everything.

Bottle labels are often laboriously handwritten, even when the prices commanded render the practice unnecessary. Packaging has become an art-form, utilizing delightful and innovative bottle

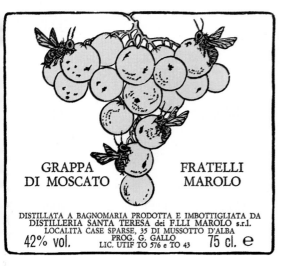

GRAPPA
DI MOSCATO

FRATELLI
MAROLO

DISTILLATA A BAGNOMARIA PRODOTTA E IMBOTTIGLIATA DA
DISTILLERIA SANTA TERESA dei F.LLI MAROLO s.r.l.
LOCALITA CASE SPARSE, 35 DI MUSSOTTO D'ALBA
PROG. G. GALLO
42% vol.    LIC. UTIF TO 576 e TO 43    75 cl. ℮

*Grappa di Moscato is produced from Muscat grapes.*

shapes, decoration and presentation. Many of the bottles are hand-blown and numbered sets are becoming collectables at silly prices. What rescues this from being just another case of skilful hype is the fact that the grappas inside these fantastic bottles are usually stunningly good.

The total grappa market in Italy is just under four million cases a year, of which just under 10% comprises the expensive 'special' and artisanal styles.

## Distillation

There is no legal prescription as to the method of distilling grappa. Both pot and continuous systems are used, as are 'bains-maries', a type of double-walled boiler that is also used elsewhere in the production of fruit brandies like kirsch, framboise and so on.

As a result of increased consumer interest in grappa in the 1960s, many producers changed over to continuous stills in order to meet demand more easily, thereby separating the purists from the rest of the pack. The distillers who were more concerned with quality chose to increase volume by putting in more pot-stills.

## Maturation

Grappa varies from non-aged to 10 years' ageing in wood. Acacia, chestnut, cherry and oak are all used for maturation, there being no legal stipulation, but young grappa is stored in inert stainless steel tanks prior to bottling to retain its pure fruit persona. Both styles are popular in Italy itself.

## Label information

The first step in controlling the 'hole-in-the-wall' image of grappa – until then somewhat akin to the illicit poteen whiskey distillation scene in Ireland – was the 1933 decree that required grappa to be bottled and display a government seal at the neck. Nevertheless, some of it would still have qualified for what Charles Dickens had in mind when he asked that a clean glass and the bottled lightning be brought forth.

Today, however, there is great enthusiasm for high-quality single-property and single-grape, or varietal, grappas, many of them with vintage dates. Considerable cachet is attached to Picolit, a fabled dessert wine whose vine has been prone to floral abortion, resulting in minimal production of grapes. Naturally, that exclusivity carries over to the grappa made from it and it is in great demand.

Consumers' tastes span from the very young to the well-aged, and have more to do with style than with price. Clear, white grappas have more in common with the fruit brandies of Alsace and are valued for just that. The diversity of grape variety, method of distillation and length of ageing make the range of grappa house-styles infinite.

'Grappa di X' will normally indicate the name of the grape(s) from which the spirit is made and not its geographical location. 'Acquavite di Vinacce' is simply an alternative term for grappa. Clear grappa sold in clear bottles will be young spirit, and aged grappa will usually be sold in bottles tinted either brown or green. Often the so-called 'international' versions of branded grappas are barrel-aged spirits which must undergo a certain minimum maturation before being permitted to go on sale in specific export markets. Most of Europe and North America now require minimum 2 years' ageing, while the UK and a number of other countries still stipulate 3 years ageing for all spirits. These regulations, originally formulated to protect consumers against crude and harmful instant distillates, are now obsolescent with today's technology.

# LISTINGS

### Bocchino

A large grappa-distiller which has managed to make some progress in exporting. The Sigillo Nero is the 'normale' but the Nebbiolo and Moscato brandies are interesting, coming from the grapes that make Barolo and Asti Spumante respectively. Cantina Privata has good weight and some intensity. All are distilled at 42% abv.

## Candolini

Fairly representative style made mostly from Friuli grapes. There is a basic range of a standard, a varietal and a de luxe. The varietal is Tokaj, which you may sample on any Alitalia flight.

### CANDOLINI TOKAJ

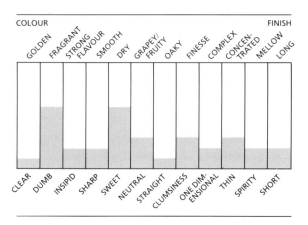

## Carpene Malvolti

This maker of sparkling wine and grape brandies (q.v.) also produces a single oak-aged grappa. Good fruit in a long finish overlaid with gently smoky woodiness. Stronger than some at 45% abv.

*Ceretto was the first company in the Langhe district to produce varietal grappas.*

## Ceretto

There are three grappas, each deriving from the pomace of, and named after, a single vineyard. Rossana is from Dolcetto grapes, delicate and quite soft, with 42% abv. Zonchera is a famous vineyard and the brandy is aromatic and velvety yet austere, with 45% abv. Brunate is the most famous vineyard of all, and the grappa is elegant and balanced, even with all of 50% abv.

A distinguished name in single-vineyard Barolo and Barbaresco wines, Ceretto was, in 1974, the first company in the Langhe district of Piedmont to produce varietal grappas. When it moved to the present site overlooking the Brunate vineyard, the old bain-marie still was carefully dismantled and re-erected on the new site. The slow distillation takes two hours and, of course, is done twice; it yields 12 litres of grappa for every five quintals (9 cwt) of pomace. Production of Zonchera and Brunate is 10 000 bottles and 1000 bottles, a year respectively.

### CERETTO ROSSANA

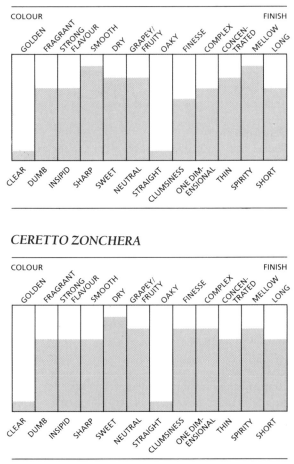

### CERETTO ZONCHERA

## CERETTO BRUNATE

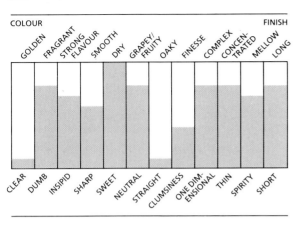

### di Gresy

The grappa produced from the Martinenga vineyard of this wine-maker has emerged as one of the top-selling brands in the United States. It is vintaged (the current year is 1985) and comes over as smooth and deep. It is achieving about 1000 cases a year in exports to the US alone, which must be close to capacity considering all the vineyard's other commitments in Barbaresco. There is also a Monte Aribaldo grappa. The Marchesi di Gresy family arrived in Turin in 1612 from Savoy and bought the Martinenga estate in the 1770s. The firm produces fine Chardonnay and new-style Barbaresco wines as well as grappa.

### Landy Frères

Landy Frères produces grappa made from pomace brought in from the DOC Piave district of Veneto to fill out the range of spirits produced by the company (see grape brandy section).

### Levi

This is the man who has done much to focus attention on grappa as something more than just a brandy. Deep in the Piedmont countryside, in a confusion of books, bottles, furniture and pet cats, Romano Levi produces grappa as an artifact. He does absolutely everything, including drawing and writing individual labels for every bottle. His spirit varies from one distillation to another – as true artisanal spirit always does – but he has a loyal following. His 'brand' is 'Grappa della Donna Selvatica che Salta le Montagne' and the labels feature in delightful colours the stick-figure of the countrywoman crossing the mountains. Levi is very shy and visits are difficult to achieve, even for his clients.

### Lungarotti

This is mainly a wine operation but the company's range of country produce includes two grappas and the distribution arrangements for the wines makes them widely accessible. The Chardonnay brandy is produced from the pomace which is taken to the distillery immediately after pressing on the firm's two estates nearby where the vine is grown. A raspberry infusion no doubt contributes to its rich bouquet of flowers and fruit. The Rubesco grappa is similarly produced from Canaiolo and Sangiovese grapes. Discontinuous stills are used and each spirit is aged for a year in oak casks.

Rubesco is a red wine created by Dottore Lungarotti in the 1960s. At a time when most Chianti had become a trashy pot-boiler of a wine, he took the Chianti grapes and showed what could be achieved with them. Rubesco had a DOC appellation (Torgiano) created around it – it was at first the only wine in the category – and it has since been promoted to the top echelon of DOCG, Italy's best.

The grappas' export markets include Canada, the United States, Britain and the main Far Eastern countries. Production is 10 000 bottles yearly. Torgiano is close to both Assisi and Perugia and the Lungarottis run a comfortable hotel called Le Tre Vaselle that is part of the Relais & Châteaux network. They organize cookery courses there and the Wine Museum in the 15th-century Palazzo Baglioni is worth a visit.

## LUNGAROTTI RUBESCO

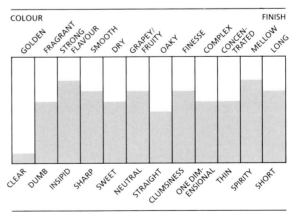

## LUNGAROTTI CHARDONNAY

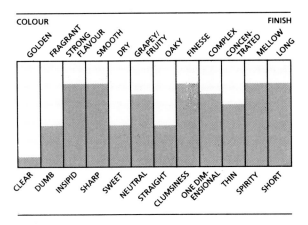

| | COLOUR | | | | | | | | | | | FINISH |
|---|---|---|---|---|---|---|---|---|---|---|---|---|
| GOLDEN | FRAGRANT | STRONG FLAVOUR | SMOOTH | DRY | GRAPEY/ FRUITY | OAKY | FINESSE | COMPLEX | CONCEN-TRATED | MELLOW | LONG | |
| CLEAR | DUMB | INSIPID | SHARP | SWEET | NEUTRAL | STRAIGHT | CLUMSINESS | ONE DIM-ENSIONAL | THIN | SPIRITY | SHORT | |

### Luxardo

The Euganean Hills near Padua in Veneto are a worthy vineyard area, giving their name to one of Italy's minor designated wines. The grapes from the region make the light, quite smooth, 40% abv Grappa Euganea. Luxardo are best known for their Sambuca and, back in 1821, were the inventors of Maraschino cherry liqueur.

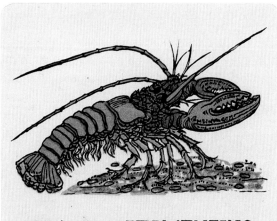

GRAPPA di VERMENTINO

*Grapes from Liguria are used in Grappa di Vermentino, a delicate grappa rich in herbaceous flavours.*

### Marolo

This is the firm that got plenty of publicity on its tenth anniversary with a commemorative Barolo grappa that cost £1200 ($2000) a bottle. One hesitates to describe an operation that produces over 20 different grappas as small, but so it is at Santa Teresa because the quantity of each is tiny. The production is artisanal but highly profession-

al, using exciting pomaces from some of Italy's greatest wines: La Scolca Gavi, Brunello Lisini, Barolo Montezemolo, the almost-extinct Arneis.

Some of the grappas are from single varieties, others from the grape-mix appropriate to a specific wine. Their distillation utilizes the bain-marie still, which is discontinuous like the pot-still, but very slow and thorough at carrying over richness of aroma and flavour in the spirit. Acacia wood as well as oak is used for ageing.

Ugo and Paolo Marolo began the business in Piedmont. Their average annual production is 25 000 bottles. Visitors to the distillery in Alba are welcome, but should telephone in advance.

The grappas are too numerous to list, but here are four tasting grids which cover a spectrum of types. The Barolo is aged for four years in acacia casks and is very strong – 54% abv; the Moscato is intense but open and zesty; the Gavi very fragrant; the distinctive Arneis is fragrant of briar-rose.

## MAROLO BAROLO

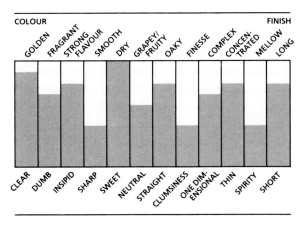

| | COLOUR | | | | | | | | | | | FINISH |
|---|---|---|---|---|---|---|---|---|---|---|---|---|
| GOLDEN | FRAGRANT | STRONG FLAVOUR | SMOOTH | DRY | GRAPEY/ FRUITY | OAKY | FINESSE | COMPLEX | CONCEN-TRATED | MELLOW | LONG | |
| CLEAR | DUMB | INSIPID | SHARP | SWEET | NEUTRAL | STRAIGHT | CLUMSINESS | ONE DIM-ENSIONAL | THIN | SPIRITY | SHORT | |

## MAROLO MOSCATO

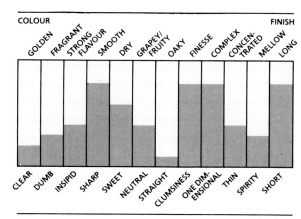

| | COLOUR | | | | | | | | | | | FINISH |
|---|---|---|---|---|---|---|---|---|---|---|---|---|
| GOLDEN | FRAGRANT | STRONG FLAVOUR | SMOOTH | DRY | GRAPEY/ FRUITY | OAKY | FINESSE | COMPLEX | CONCEN-TRATED | MELLOW | LONG | |
| CLEAR | DUMB | INSIPID | SHARP | SWEET | NEUTRAL | STRAIGHT | CLUMSINESS | ONE DIM-ENSIONAL | THIN | SPIRITY | SHORT | |

*Grappa di Barolo, an austere, highly aromatic grappa, is distilled in a* bain-marie *and aged for almost 4 years in small acacia wood casks.*

## MAROLO GAVI LA SCOLCA

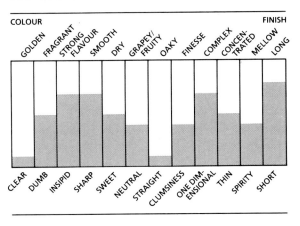

## MAROLO ARNEIS

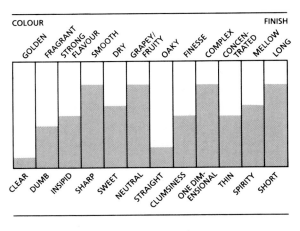

### Masi

An important producer of popular Veneto wines and limited bottlings of Recioto from small individual vineyards. Many of these yield rich pomace which is now being assessed for the production of different grappas. Those already made from Campolongo Torbe and Mezzanella are rounded and well-finished from up to five years' ageing in oak and/or acacia casks.

### Montagliari

A smooth and rounded artisanal grappa distilled from grapes of the Chianti Classico vineyard of Montagliari in Tuscany. It is oak-aged and the bottles are individually numbered. The vineyard also produces excellent vin santo.

### Nannoni

High-quality grappa from a pleasantly eccentric specialist producer. This small artisanal grappa distillery claims to have invented Tuscan grappa. They have a steam-heated pot-still and distil all pomace within 24 hours of its arrival at the distillery. Even non-fermented pomace is fermented and distilled within five days. The spirits age in small casks made from an extraordinarily wide range of wood including wild cherry, pear, apple, chestnut and six different types of oak.

### Nardini

An upmarket name in grappa production, Nardini recognized the potential in fine grappa when no-one else produced it on any great scale. Today, although it holds its own in the premium sector, there is a lot of competition and more imaginative marketing to contend with. Its spirits are all 'acquavite', a formal term which, certainly initially, set them apart from the rough and industrial grappas that mainly constituted the market 20 years ago. Double-distilled and high-strength, Nardini grappas are straight and classic in style. The firm dates from 1779 when Bartolo Nardini settled in, appropriately, Bassano del Grappa.

*The pride, artistry and attention to detail of the small producer are evident in these hand-blown bottles from Nonino, a leading name in the grappa market.*

### Nonino

An innovative specialist distillery that began in 1886 when Grandpa Nonino wheeled his mobile distillery from village to village in Friuli.

After much experimentation, the company has found that small casks of wild cherry wood are best for the grappas it produces and that the whole-grape Ue spirit it 'invented' shows well in different woods. This is a family firm in the fullest sense; Benito Nonino, his beautiful wife and three daughters all work *con amore* in the business.

In 1967 they started taking pomace from important individual vineyards and in 1973 the first varietal grappa came off the stills. The Noninos instigated an annual award to encourage growers to plant near-extinct local vines.

So successful was the project that the Italian government subsequently first authorized, then recommended, these grapes for distillation. It also authorized Ue, a new category of spirit the Noninos devised. It is made from distilling whole grapes – a combination of brandy (where the juice ferments) and grappa (where the pomace does so).

These are made in a separate little distillery in the old forge where Benito's father-in-law used to make ploughs, and the bottles are hand-blown by a Murano glassmaker. An American paid £1200 ($2000) for a first-run 1984 bottle and a German paid £4800 ($8000) for the complete range of four! Distillers from France, Germany and Austria regularly visit the distillery to study the methods of working there. There are now 24 discontinuous stills in the main distillery and 12 in the little one.

Demand exceeds supply but Nonino exports to Germany, the United States and Britain. It is probably the leading name in production at this top end of the grappa market.

Visitors are welcome but should telephone ahead.

### NONINO OPTIMA

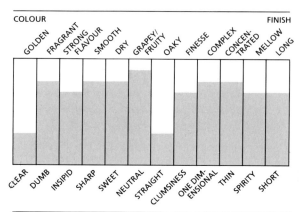

### NONINO PICOLIT

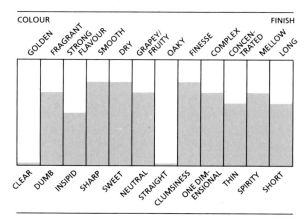

### NONINO GEWÜRZTRAMINER

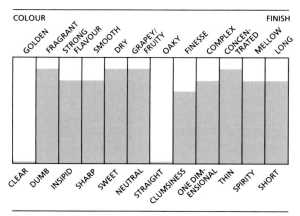

## Stock

Grappa Julia is probably the grappa brand-leader in Italy. It is distilled by a large number of small operators during the harvest time, when the pomace is fresh, and Stock buys the spirit in from them; it has the capacity needed for the turnover of large quantities and the extra ageing required for export grappa brands like Julia. The grappa matures in stainless steel for a minimum of two years before going on sale and is consistent from year to year. Julia Bianca is an unaged, clear grappa with a fresh clean scent and zesty fruit pungency.

Stock are probably responsible for the early stages of the now world-wide awareness of grappa, at least as a product associated with Italy. Their excellent international distribution for the vast range of other spirits and liqueurs gave continuing opportunities to place Grappa Julia in good outlets around the world. Grappa Julia in the distinctive brown bottle with nipped-in waist is by far the most widely available grappa.

## Villa Colonna

Two interesting varietal grappas are at the sharp end of this company, which has been doing quite a bit of promotion to increase distribution of its range of spirits, including a 1974 vintage grape XO brandy. There is a Chardonnay grappa and a clear grappa from pomace of Brunello di Montalcino, an absolute top-rank red wine from Tuscany. It is attractively packaged in a spherical 'bomb' bottle.

*(Above) Lungarotti Rubesco is a grappa produced from a high quality wine of the same name.*

*(Above) Grappa Julia, the leading grappa in Italy, is distilled to the specifications of Stock by a large number of small operators.*

*(Top) A splendid Morolo anniversary bottle.*

# UNITED STATES OF AMERICA

How do you get from the gentle activities of the monks planting vines to make sacramental wine in their mission vineyards up and down the west coast of America to the civic unrest inflicted by the Chicago gangster mobs? The answer is you introduce Prohibition and dislocate the lives and livelihoods of a generation of Americans. You also create the circumstances whereby accomplished cognoscenti like Bugs Moran and Al Capone become your neighbourhood suppliers, each carrying out in-trade promotional incentives like the St Valentine's Day massacre in 1929.

Before Prohibition Americans knew their wines and appreciated the high quality of their domestic product, but after 13 years of 'the long thirst' they had lost their palate. The growers, too, had changed things, replacing classic wine grapes in the vineyards with those that would sell as table grapes or best serve the bootleggers' requirements.

As a result, the awful wines made in sour wood from unsuitable grapes after repeal not surprisingly did not sell and soon grape surpluses looked like purple and green mountain ranges.

What a contrast this was to the situation in 1623, when the colonial assembly in Virginia passed a law requiring every family unit to plant 10 vines on its land. Because of phylloxera, European vines that the early settlers had brought with them always failed and the settlers drank cider and applejack instead of wine and brandy.

Although native grape species yielded wine in various locations, the first successful non-local vines came into the United States from Mexico in the 1770s, as the Franciscan friars established their line of mission stations up the length of California. The oldest winery in California is thought to be the San Gabriel mission, near Los Angeles, which was built in 1771 and where Indians trod the grapes for the brothers' wine-making.

In 1842, Captain John Sutter, the Swiss immigrant who founded Sacramento, was known to be distilling brandy from local wild grapes in his fort at the settlement. Six years later the Gold Rush

*The Gewürztraminer vineyards of Paul Masson at Soledad, Monterey County, California.*

began, and it played its part in establishing vineyards in California. Many of those who did not make a strike turned to making wine and brandy, and did very well out of doing so. This created a 'grape rush' and, with tax exemptions on new vineyards, grape-production broke out all over the state from the 1850s onwards.

Three important transatlantic events took place in the 1860s and 1870s. Some time in 1862, the phylloxera aphid was apparently exported from the United States to Europe. It was first noticed on a sample vine which turned up in 1863 in Hammersmith, London, although the first vineyards to suffer were in the south of France.

The Cognac area was hit in the 1870s and the supply of brandy soon began to dry up. The distillers of southern Spain were not affected until the 1890s, but eventually the entire European vineyard was destroyed over a 30-year period.

However, having given the Old World the cold, American know-how also furnished the cure. Throughout the 1870s, Dr Thomas Munson of Red River, Texas, and Hermann Jaeger of Missouri supplied Europe with louse-resistant American vine-roots on to which European vines could be grafted; as a result, France awarded them the Légion d'Honneur.

While this rescue was under way, William Thompson of Yuba City introduced a new grape variety to California. He gave his name to an English vine he had acquired when he planted it on his farm in 1872; the Thompson Seedless was to become famous for over-production as well as brandy-production.

Just a year later phylloxera broke out in Napa, Sonoma and several other valleys in California and it took nearly 30 years to eradicate. (Unhappily, during the 1980s a new strain of the disease to which the mainstay rootstock has no resistance has been spreading throughout the same areas. It is believed that replanting is likely to be the only longterm solution.)

By the end of the 19th century American wines had developed to the point of picking up competition gold medals at the Paris Expositions of 1876 and 1900. Paradoxically, by this time three American states had already gone dry, and in the event it was to be another 40 years before quality brandy-production in the United States resumed in the wake of the repeal of Prohibition.

# GRAPE BRANDY

## The countryside

The city of Lodi is the fulcrum of the wine and brandy industry that lies close to the delta of the San Joaquin River. It is flat land striped with endless rows of vines, many of which grow to extraordinary height and girth. Walking the rows is more like being in an orchard rather than in a vineyard. The delta's rivers, creeks and baylets dominate the appearance of the landscape as well as affecting the microclimate. Flame Tokay is the main grape here.

South along the San Joaquin Valley, the scale of operation becomes enormous across the flat, irrigated, richly fertile plain. Thompson Seedless are everywhere and can crop more than 16 tonnes to a half hectare (16 tons to the acre). Almost all California brandy derives from here.

## History

American wine-making evolved well during the 19th century and the honest but inconsistent California brandy was good enough to be shipped in considerable quantities to Europe in the 1880s to replace the cognac that was no longer available due to phylloxera infestation of the vineyards.

From the 1840s onwards many of the vineyard-owners in California were also distilling brandy, but it was Leland Stanford, Senator and former Governor of California, who put brandy spectacularly in the spotlight. He bought and extended the Vina property in Tehama County and the brandy he made there became so successful that he quickly became the world's largest brandy-distiller.

Stanford sold to New York and elsewhere and when he died the business was left to Stanford University at Palo Alto. Brandy sales helped subsidize the university until growing Prohibitionist pressure forced its administrators to break up the estate and sell it off.

Prohibition was a watershed for the wine and brandy industry; it constituted an almost complete hiatus for the former and the effective starting point for the latter.

In California, three of the five grape harvests immediately following the repeal of Prohibition were massive. Half of the 2½ million-ton crop in 1938, mainly Thompson Seedless, was designated overproduction. In the same year, an emergency grape prorate was voted in the state, requiring every producer to distil 45% of his crop into brandy and store it for two years.

During the Second World War, these stores of brandy – by now maturing nicely – were assessed by experienced brandy-makers from Europe and from them a prototype California brandy was 'designed' that was lighter than the famous French brandies and different in aroma and flavour.

After the war, distilleries too were designed specifically to make the new style of brandy and it was instantly popular. By the end of the 1960s, brandy consumption had risen four-fold in the United States and 75% of it was the new Californian product.

## The brandy

Occasionally today you will see an old-timer pick up a bottle of brandy and automatically turn it upside down for no apparent reason. Sixty years ago, it was done to see if there was any sediment in the bottle, an unwanted feature that would give a clue as to how the brandy tasted.

The filtering and general preparation of beverages is taken for granted today, but the presence of sulphur in wines used for distillation was a big problem before the war. Apart from the nasty tastes and smells of sulphur and vinegar it imparted to the brandy, it also caused metal to flake off the inside of the still to form the sediment, and sulphuric acid to form in the bottle.

The 'heads' – the first-run part of the distillate – was never separated from the main body of spirit before the war, and this contributed another group of unpleasant smells and flavours to some brandy. Iron contamination during wood-ageing often occurred, too, causing blue/green discoloration in the spirit. Even wholesome brandy tended to be uneven in style because continuous stills needed monitoring and manual control of both the in-flow and out-flow pipes, and variations in either changed the nature of the spirit going through.

So, without any long-entrenched traditions for the brandy-makers to draw on, there was a lot to learn in terms of attitude, expertise and technique, and it is to the eternal credit of the industry that it was able to tackle so much from scratch after the war and get it right first time.

Trade leaders like A. R. Morrow, L. K. Marshall and E. B. Brown did most in the drive for high quality, and the industry grew at a healthy 8% average for the next 15 years, enabling it to become firmly established.

By the 1960s, production and stocks were doubling every five years. The attitude of distillers improved out of all recognition, and became identifiable with the country's better wine-makers, now famous worldwide for their commitment to the integrity of their product. An important result of this is today's growing and harvesting of grapes specifically aimed at brandy-making.

Once all the problems had been sorted out, a brandy emerged that was, and is, clean, light and appealing to a wide range of tastes, and which does not need much ageing before going on sale. Fine tuning in production styles may be achieved without resorting to pot-stills by changing the configuration of the still to produce at lower strength, using very high-quality distilling wines and maturing the brandy longer.

## Grapes

When the new Californian breed of brandy was created after the war, most of the grapes used were Thompson Seedless from the San Joaquin Valley in the great Fresno-Bakersfield belt.

Growers liked Thompsons because they offered three market options – table grapes, raisins or wine-making. When the question of also using them for brandy arose, studies showed that when Thompsons' acidity/sugar balance was right it was a splendid grape for brandy-making anyway, so growers gained a fourth option and a means of dealing with overproduction.

Emperor grapes are also widespread in that area, while further north, at Lodi, Flame Tokay was the main vine. The cognac/armagnac grapes, Ugni Blanc, Colombard and Folle Blanche, have always been used very successfully by small California producers following French production precepts and their cultivation continues to extend. Some producers have even managed to tone down the acidity of the Ugni Blanc grape and make pleasant wine from it, but one of them withdrew his brand when customers habitually described it as 'Ugly Blank'.

## Distillation

All the distilleries making the post-war California style of brandy use continuous stills but several makers are doing more individualistic things with copper pot-stills. Most aim at a distillation strength of 80–85% abv, pitched to give short-term aged spirits a smoother, less pungent texture by taking off certain low oils in the boiling. Brandies aimed at longer ageing are collected at 70–75% abv.

One of the reasons pre-war brandies were generally so poor is that brandy grapes were always last to be processed. Often distillation went on into February and sulphur dioxide had to be used to protect stocks from spoiling, something that is proscribed in world brandy-making these days since the smell and flavour always comes over in the spirit.

In 1939, there were 101 continuous stills of various makes operating in California including De Valle, Sanders, Ergot, Hebert and Barbet. Krenz single-column stills seemed more popular in northern California and Pacific double-column units in the south. There were only ten pot-stills.

Copper is a singularly appropriate metal for distillation because it scavenges sulphur compounds out of the spirit, and when stainless steel stills were introduced, some copper metal was usually incorporated inside the vessel to carry out this function.

## Maturation

In 1941 the authorities put a ceiling of 85% abv on distillation strength if the spirit was to avoid being categorized as 'neutral'. In the 1930s there had been a wide range of cask strengths – from 60% to 95% abv – and the new regulation meant that the first of the new brandies were simply high-strength examples reduced with water to about 50% abv and briefly aged in oak casks.

The Korbel Tower, Sonoma County, California.

This was exactly what the law was supposed to prevent, but quite quickly the practice was dropped in favour of correct treatments. The distillation strengths were brought much lower but the ageing strength of around 50% abv was retained.

On the other hand, 50% abv is very close to the 40% abv strength at which brandy is now marketed, which means that over several years of maturation in wood a high proportion of the ageing liquid is just water!

Barrels were new – used ones would have little tempering effect on the more fiery spirits – and many were also charred, but by far the majority of them were plain white oak.

Today, the situation has completely turned round. New charred oak is no longer used and barrels that have previously held bourbon or brandy are much in demand for the nuance and gentler influences they impart.

Although French Limousin oak passes on more actual wood extract to a distillate than American white oak, its impact is less marked and the effect is softer and subtler.

The minimum ageing of two years is now as it was before the war, but most blends will also incorporate spirits of 8–12 years. Brandy today mostly sells at 40% abv (80% Proof American) – the legal minimum – instead of 45% abv prewar.

## Label information

American labelling demands great frankness on the part of the bottlers. If the product is from lees, residue or dried fruit, or is neutral or substandard, whichever word applies must be put before the word 'brandy' on the label. The only exceptions in the whole brandy category are applejack, grappa and cognac, the generic names of which are allowed to be self-explanatory.

Several US brandy-makers have been interested lately in using oak chips in the preparation of their spirit, and there has been protracted debate at official level as to whether all brandies, including cognac, should bear labels in the United States stating that they have been 'coloured and flavoured with wood chips'.

After three years of deliberation, the authorities have declared that it will be decided from the strength of submitted oak infusions whether each individual brandy-producer should declare use of boisé on the bottle labels. All such colouring, flavouring or blending materials – which include local cream 'sherry' and prune juice – are limited to 2.5% volume of the finished brandy.

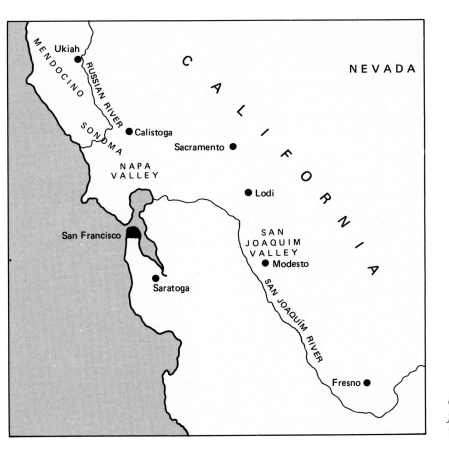

*Californian vineyards account for 75% of brandy consumed in the United States.*

## Places to visit

San Francisco could be a holiday in itself with its bustle, colour and vibrancy. Go to Union Square, Nob Hill, Fisherman's Wharf, and Mission Dolores which was founded in the same year as the Revolution.

Ghirardelli Square is named for the chocolate-seller whose famous parrot both advertised his goods and corrected people's pronunciation of his name – it simply kept on repeating 'Ghirardelli, Ghirardelli' with the hard 'G'. You should also see The Cannery, Pier 39 and try a few cable-car rides.

Guided tours of Alcatraz leave from the Embarcadero – a haunting experience. After all those atmospheric old movies you feel it should all be in black and white. It was originally a lighthouse point and first held prisoners during the Civil War.

Four or five of the famous brandy distilleries lie north of San Francisco. Heading there, you have the option of stopping off at the Marine World oceanarium at Vallejo and Jack London's Waterfront with the famous bar he loved, the First and Last Chance saloon.

You can visit Napa on the Wine Train, restored and reinstated to stop at three stations including St Helena, where Christian Brothers produce wine and brandy at Mont La Salle. Robert Louis Stevenson lived near there in the 1880s and his writings about Silverado made it famous. There are memorabilia in the museum.

Quaint Calistoga has hot springs and mud baths and, nearby, the 'Old Faithful' geyser erupts every 45 minutes. There is also a 'petrified' forest of redwood trees which was encased in ash from the 1860 eruption of Mount St Helena. The RMS distillery is located here and is particularly interesting due to its French-style distillation and experimentation with different European grapes.

Off Highway 101 are the Muir Woods, a stand of Sequoia redwood trees which reach 76 m (250 ft) in height.

San Rafael was the penultimate mission in the chain of 21, and the town is today surrounded by vineyards. Another cognac-style brandy is produced here by Russell Woodbury.

General Vallejo's 1834 rancho at Petaluma gives a good idea of life in California during the days of Mexican rule. There is a Historic Park devoted to Jack London at Glen Ellen where he used to live and write, and Santa Rosa has a museum that is a memorial to Robert Ripley, originator of the 'Believe-It-Or-Not' strip.

Russian colonists gave their name to Russian River and the shore road offers beautiful touring country. Guerneville hosts the Korbel cellars, famous for both their brandy and their sparkling wine made by the champagne method.

Further north are the arresting Trinity Alps and Willow Creek is where Bigfoot, the giant apeman, is said to live.

East of San Francisco lies Sacramento; the old part, with its cobbled streets and wooden sidewalks, lies prettily alongside the river. It is now a national park. Sacramento boomed during the Gold Rush and the History Centre has a lot of interesting exhibits from that era. Next door is the enormous Historic Railroad Museum, with its extraordinary collection of restored trains and railroad equipment.

The Towe Ford Museum has every Ford model and year from 1903 to 1953. The State Indian Museum and a reconstruction of the original Sutter's Fort settlement are close by.

East of Sacramento lies the Mother Lode, the stretch of country where gold was discovered in 1848 and the Gold Rush began. Over 90 000 'forty-niners' poured into the area and today you can travel along – appropriately – Highway 49 to see a whole succession of interesting Gold Rush sites.

Quaint little Coloma was the first boom-town and is preserved as part of the Marshall State Park. British visitors to Nevada City will be intrigued to enjoy apparently genuine Cornish pasties, a local speciality established in Gold Rush days when a party of former Cornish tin-miners settled in to the area.

In Grass Valley, the Empire Mine has become a historic park and the house of Lola Montez, where she lived with a pet bear, still stands on Mill Street. Mokelumne Hill still has its 1850s architecture and Placerville had so many 'necktie parties' that they used to call it Hangtown. Grinding Rock has interesting Miwok petroglyphs in the Indian Historic Park there.

Throughout the Mother Lode there are old courthouses, saloons, former mines and numerous gold-mine museums to visit, all with the looks and the feel of those raucous bygone days.

A drive up 2133 m (7000 ft)-high Echo Summit suddenly reveals shimmering lake Tahoe set in the midst of the High Sierra mountains. The lake is a focal point for holidaymakers and fishing, hiking, bicycling, golfing, horse-riding and skiing are all catered for. Accommodation is plentiful.

## GRAPE BRANDY LISTINGS
### Alambic

Two enthusiasts in partnership are engaged in hand-producing small quantities of artisanal brandy from an antique still brought over to Mendocino County from Cognac. Hubèrt Germain-Robin hails from the Robin dynasty that has been making cognac since 1782, and Ansley Coale is a former academic from Princeton, New Jersey.

The partners use a painstaking method of production which originated in Cognac but is now largely obsolete due to its expensive and time-consuming routine. Grapes used are Colombard, Pinot Noir and Gamay, Mendocino-grown varietals; cellaring is in Limousin oak.

There is an unusual complexity in the brandy that derives from the unusual grape mix, and apparently the premium grapes used require less ageing. Fruit quality is good, with fresh grape flavours and overall finesse.

The brandies have outshone several extremely prestigious cognac brands in a series of blind tastings put on by the proprietors. Their Réserve was served at a White House gala dinner given in honour of the Soviet First Family, the Gorbachevs, when they visited the United States.

### Labels
Germain-Robin VSOP 6yo; Germain-Robin Réserve.

*Alambic Inc. brandies, produced by traditional methods, compare favourably with venerable brand leaders.*

## GERMAIN-ROBIN VSOP

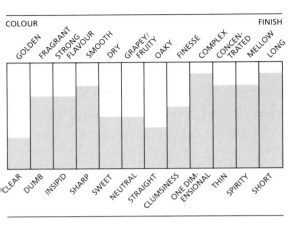

## GERMAIN-ROBIN RÉSERVE

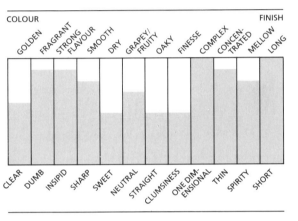

*Christian Brothers vineyards, founded by a French Catholic teaching order, began producing wine and spirits in the Napa Valley in the late nineteenth century.*

In 1989, the Brothers withdrew from the brandy business and the firm was sold to the giant British firm Grand Metropolitan. This brought to an end a long tradition of wine- and brandy-making by the French Roman Catholic teaching order. At the tail-end of last century, they made their first wine by using wooden clubs to bash grapes to a fermenting pulp in a horse-trough.

The Brothers owned a number of wineries and vineyards, but the focal point was always the lovely setting of the Mount Veeder slopes in Napa County, with the monastery and the winery side-by-side amid the vineyards.

### Labels
Jacques Bonet; Christian Brothers XO 5/8yo.

### Christian Brothers

Christian Brothers' brandy position as best-seller in the United States has been usurped by Gallo's E & J, but it still sells very great amounts in second place. The brandy is made from both pot-stills and unusual four-columned continuous stills; the extra columns' function is to clean out aldehydes from the spirit.

Colombard, Thomson Seedless and Chenin Blanc grapes are used although, at a distillation strength of just under 85% abv, fruit characteristics only, with no grape-type individuality, are all that will come over.

The XO is a 'cognac-type' brandy made half from the continuously-distilled spirit and half from very simple, kettle-like copper pot-stills particular to the Christian Brothers who developed them. The XO is oak-aged for up to eight years. The Jacques Bonet name is a new label acquired to market a lesser, sweeter brandy.

## CHRISTIAN BROTHERS XO

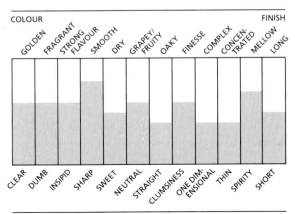

*E & J is the largest selling brandy in the US; its lightness and smoothness make it an excellent mixer.*

## Gallo

Gallo first marketed their brandy in 1968 and eventually took over from the Christian Brothers as the leading United States brand in the early 1980s. E & J is not, and is not intended to be, a sipping brandy; its lightness and smoothness allow it to be all things to most people. Spirit is drawn off the continuous stills quite high up the strength scale. It is then aged in different batches for from three to 12 years in charred, seasoned American white oak barrels. These are then blended in proportions which aim for lightness with just enough older brandy to establish brandy identity and avoid over-assertiveness.

The ageing process is always meant to mellow out a spirit, but to safeguard the final smoothness, E & J is charcoal-filtered before bottling.

Both smell and taste of E & J are light and often fleeting, but this non-assertiveness certainly makes E & J an excellent mixing brandy, a role for which it seems ideally suited. Gallo put no flavourings or sweetening in their brandy.

We're talking big here – the company owns the world's biggest winery and supplies a quarter of the wine consumed in the United States. Gallo produces half of the wine that comes out of California in addition to producing the country's top-selling brandy.

While they were still students in Modesto, California, the Gallo brothers, Ernest and Julio, waited for Prohibition to end in 1933 so that they could set up a winery. From the local public

library they unearthed some 'how to' wine-making documentation that had been published before Prohibition. Their first batch turned out OK and they set to work producing wines for everyday use at keen prices.

When the company took a stride up-market in 1974, one journalist wrote of the firm's doing 'something wholly unprecedented in its 40-year history – it put a cork in a bottle of Gallo wine.'

Progression beyond screwtop mass wines has been achieved and the 50 wines they now market, some under various sous-marques, range from the slightest to the very finest. They have always been innovative, usually got things right and just kept on growing.

The brothers are diffident, however, regarding the public and none of their many sites is open to visitors. The highly visible winery at Modesto, with its vast array of storage tanks, looks like an oil refinery. There are no signs or posters to indicate that it is not.

### Label
Gallo E & J Brandy 3/12yo.

### GALLO E & J

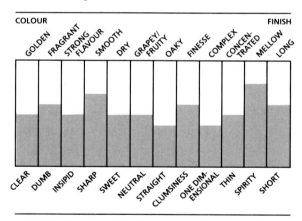

### Guild

This is a co-operative owned by over 300 Californian grape-growers which, until recently, marketed a range of excellent combined pot- and continuous still brandies. They have now withdrawn from brandy-production to concentrate exclusively on their range of wines. Cook's, their main constituent brand, has the macabre distinction of having been once owned by Hitler's foreign minister, von Ribbentrop. You may still come across the odd bottle or two, but if you like them buy them up because they're likely to be the last you ever see. The Cresta Blanca was made from 100% Flame Tokay and was the first American brandy to carry a vintage date, that of 1966.

## Labels

Cribari; Guild; Ceremony; St. Mark's; Cresta Blanca.

## CRESTA BLANCA

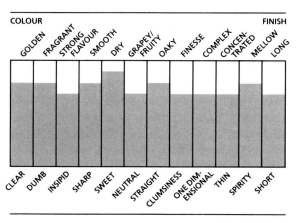

## Jepson

The brandy is the first release from a small distillery set up in 1983 using one of only three genuine Charentais pot-stills in use in California. The brandy is totally integral to the estate 'from bud-break to bottle', the Colombard grapes coming from 110 acres of vines on the 1200-acre ranch at Ukiah, California.

*Jepson Brandy, produced in genuine Charentais pot-stills, has a distinctive style of its own.*

The vines grow on the banks of the Russian River and are quite mature, about 30-years-old. The brandy has a distinctive style of its own, with more fruit presence than the cognacs it may well be compared with.

This interesting new operation is owned by Robert Jepson, a Chicago industrialist, and worked by an impassioned brandy-maker called Rick Jones. He trained at the famous Davis viticultural college in California where the beautiful little pilot distillery entranced him sufficiently to lure him into detailed work with it.

On graduation, he went straight into distilling and spent a month visiting several different firms in Cognac. Sparkling wines are also produced by Jepson and the vines include Chardonnay and Chenin Blanc. Jones has already distilled some Chardonnay as a first move towards producing eaux-de-vie from different grape-types.

## Label

Jepson Brandy 5/6yo.

## JEPSON BRANDY

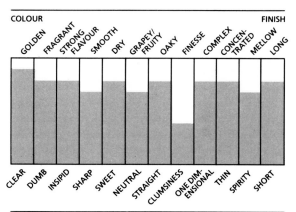

*The 100 year-old Korbel winery building.*

## Korbel

The brandy is produced from continuous stills, but the distillation is contracted out to a specialist company who carry out the process to Korbel's specifications. Although this renders the grape-types used less important, they are, for the record, Colombard, Chenin Blanc and Flame Tokay, all of which are bought in from the Central Valley.

Korbel aim for a smooth, light brandy with the accent on fruit persona. Interestingly, they mature their brandy by using a solera blending system, based on that used in Jerez, Spain (q.v.). There are 15 successive oak tanks of spirit, each of which is half-emptied when movements are made. This is done four-to-six times a year.

This is absolutely unique in California. With the above rate of progression through the solera, the brandy is usually 3 to 4 years-old when it is bottled. The extra richness from solera ageing makes Korbel's brandy suitable for both sipping and mixing.

As Czech immigrants, the Korbels began making brandy in 1892 and built up a successful business. In 1954 the firm was sold to the Heck family, originally from Alsace. Korbel sparkling wines are well-known throughout the United States. They are made by the champagne method and Korbel have been making them this way longer than anyone else in the USA.

### KORBEL BRANDY

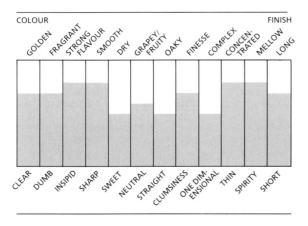

In the 1960s, they invented a machine that displaced the famous 'lift-and-twist' process that shifts the fermentation lees into the neck of the bottle.

### Label

Korbel Brandy 3/4yo.

*Korbel brandy is produced using the 'solera' system, which accelerates the ageing of spirits in barrel.*

## Paul Masson

Both continuous and 20000-litre pot-stills are used in the production of this high-volume brandy, up to 15% of pot spirit going into the standard blend. The grapes are usually Colombard and distillation strength is close to that of cognac at 72.5% abv. This is brought down to about 58% abv for the three-year ageing period in small American oak barrels.

Masson maintains about 19 000 barrels in a controlled environment where the humidity is high and the floors are kept wet to reduce strength in the barrels at what the cellar-master feels is the optimum rate for the company house-style. Masson is a 'typical' Californian brandy – aimed at being mellow, easy-to-drink and round with a woodiness to its flavour. The company produce a range of de-alcoholized wines, and much of the extracted alcohol is added to the brandy spirit. One half of 1 percent of sugar syrup is added before bottling.

*Paul Masson's Pinnacles Winery, Soledad, California*

Paul Masson emigrated to California in 1878 from Burgundy when his family's 300-year-old vineyards were wiped out by phylloxera. There, he teamed up with another Frenchman to produce 'champagne' which was good enough to win awards at many international competitions. He created a remarkable 'vineyard in the sky' on steep slopes in the Santa Cruz Mountains near Saratoga. The vineyard is now a protected monument.

During prohibition, he succeeded in having one of his wines officially designated as 'medicinal champagne'! The stone-built winery has a 12th-century Spanish Romanesque portal and musical concerts are regularly held in this lovely setting. The Champagne Cellars in Saratoga are well-geared to receive visitors and the winery architecture is striking.

### Label
Paul Masson Brandy

### PAUL MASSON BRANDY

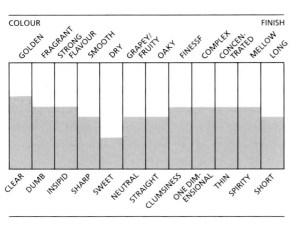

## RMS

This is brandy produced in the same way as cognac, using authentic cognac stills and financed by one of the big names in cognac distillation, Rémy Martin. There are eight stills and the five grape-types used are distilled separately. They are Colombard, Pinot Noir, Muscat, Chenin Blanc and Palomino. After distillation they also age for two years separately before being blended to mature further in Limousin casks.

The final brandy spends a minimum of five years ageing in oak before sale and the brand has been on the market now for three years.

### Label
RMS Brandy 5yo.

## Royal Host

Crown Regency is the top brand from this co-operative of 300 members. It is a straight brandy with no flavouring cordials added to it. In blind tastings, it has often competed against VSOPs and XOs from three of the very well-known cognac brands and has acquitted itself well.

The other two brandies are blended. Royal Host has prune cordial and sugar syrup added to it, while Mission Host is rounded out with cream 'sherry'.

A large proportion of the growers in the co-operative are of German origin. They use a copper continuous still that was built in the 1930s to make the spirit and, being located at Lodi, they cultivate Flame Tokay grapes for their distillation wines.

### Labels
Crown Regency XOS 8/20yo straight; Royal Host 3/8yo blended; Mission Host 2yo blended.

*Crown Regency brandy is produced in continuous copper stills. There are no flavouring cordials added, and in blind tastings, Crown Regency scored higher than a number of top-of-the-market cognacs.*

### CROWN REGENCY XOS

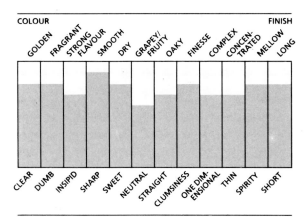

### Vie-Del

Vie-Del in Fresno are specialist distillers who produce spirit to order for many of the well-known brand-owners on the US market. They maintain the largest stocks of brandy in the world, with 15 million gallons in thousands of oak casks. Not all of this is for their own label; much of the contract brandy produced for clients also ages here.

## POMACE BRANDY – GRAPPA

Consumer interest in grappa has been growing recently in the United States (see Italian chapter for production details). There seems to be no specific reason other than curiosity in a product that many people had heard mentioned in conversation but had never actually tasted. Even third or fourth generation Italian Americans stay closely in touch with their cultural roots and it would be hard to find an Italian restaurant in any part of the world that would not have at least a representative bottle of grappa on the bar shelf.

Consider, too, the fact that Italians are a social and effusive race – there are many occasions when regular customers are offered something different to sip after a good meal. The restaurateur at the Bella Voce in San Francisco even has '1 GRAPPA' as his car number-plate.

Such is the growth of interest in this brandy that a number of wine-makers have started to study it and already there are a few Californian examples. At least one producer has elected to follow the French style of pomace brandy, calling his spirit marc. Wine-awareness has meant that a lot of attention is being paid to varietal grappas and this is the direction being followed by these new Californian brandy producers.

## LISTINGS

### Bonny Doon

Isabella is a labrusca vine which lends itself to distillation and is intensely aromatic. Niagara is also a labrusca plant, although it is not as clearly delineated as the other. Muscat is usually aromatic in whichever guise it appears.

Randall Grahm set up this small distillery and is experimenting with all sorts of possibilities for grappas and fruit brandies. He is new to distillation but does not lack ideas or energy. He and his partner have been working on the grappas for a year and a half, and they have visited Italy to consult leading distillers like Nonino and Pojer & Sandri.

### Labels

Niagara Grappa; Isabella Grappa; Muscat Grappa.

### BONNY DOON NIAGARA GRAPPA

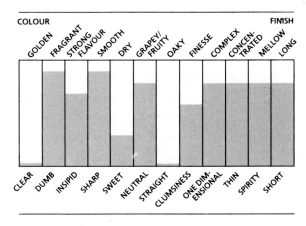

### Clear Creek

This is a small distillery run by Stephen McCarthy and his brothers that makes grappa and eaux-de-vie by methods used in the Black Forest, Alsace and Switzerland. The pot-stills are small and were manufactured in Germany.

The grappa is distilled from Muscat Ottonel pomace deriving from The Eyrie vineyards of David Lett in Oregon. McCarthy adds a little yeast to help things along, and his grappa is noticeably aromatic. The distillery operates on the best artisanal lines and their brandies are highly thought of, usually emerging on top in blind testings.

# CLEAR CREEK DISTILLERY

*Label*
Muscat Ottonel Grappa.

### CLEAR CREEK MUSCAT OTTONEL GRAPPA

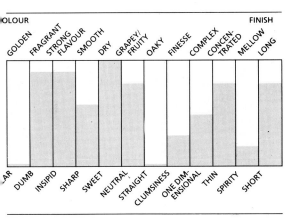

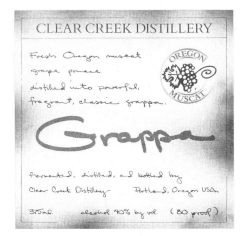

*Muscat Ottonel Grappa – from local Oregon vineyards.*

### Creekside

This is a recently-established distillery run by Don Johnson in Gordon Valley, Solano County, an hour's drive from San Francisco. While wine-makers in several countries make port from Cabernet Sauvignon, I have never come across a brandy from this grape. Don Johnson, however, has started making a grappa from Cabernet Sauvignon pomace.

*Label*
Cabernet Sauvignon Grappa.

### CREEKSIDE CABERNET SAUVIGNON GRAPPA

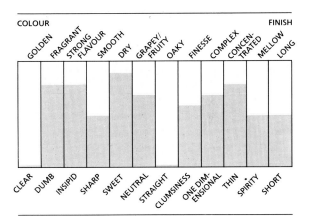

### St. George Spirits

This distillery's innovative proprietor, Jorg Rupf, uses Zinfandel pomace to produce a true grappa-style brandy. Using an aromatic Gewürztraminer, he makes what he calls a 'marc', but which is really what the Italian producer, Nonino, calls 'Ue'. This is made with whole grapes, combining intensity and faithful rendering of the grape's flavour.

### GEWÜRTZTRAMINER MARC

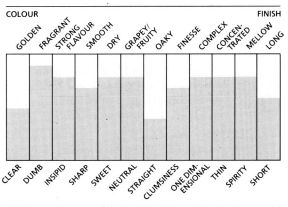

## ST. GEORGE SPIRITS ZINFANDEL GRAPPA

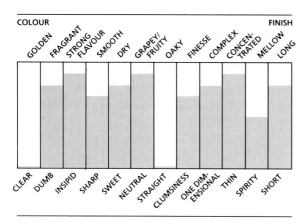

| COLOUR | | | | | | | | | | | | FINISH |
|--------|--|--|--|--|--|--|--|--|--|--|--|--------|
| GOLDEN | FRAGRANT | STRONG FLAVOUR | SMOOTH | DRY | GRAPEY/ FRUITY | OAKY | FINESSE | COMPLEX | CONCEN-TRATED | MELLOW | LONG | |
| CLEAR | DUMB | INSIPID | SHARP | SWEET | NEUTRAL | STRAIGHT | CLUMSINESS | ONE DIM-ENSIONAL | THIN | SPIRITY | SHORT | |

# FRUIT BRANDY – APPLEJACK/APPLE BRANDY

The backwoods way of making applejack was to leave containers of the fermented mixture outdoors in winter-time so that the water froze and left neater and neater apple-flavoured alcohol the longer you waited.

The trouble was that what you got was the whole poisonous package with all the well-tried headache-makers in it – no heads or tails cut out for you.

It is much better to have an effective, slow-boiling still concentrate the flavours and surrender a wholesome heart of the run to you. On the other hand the early stills used by settlers in Virginia and New Jersey were not wholly satisfactory. 'Jersey Lightning' was the name given to the apple brandy produced which tended to cause a condition called 'Apple Palsy'.

Today, applejack is produced in a similar way to France's calvados (q.v.), namely as a double-distilled spirit from pot-stills.

The first cider-distillation produces a brouillis of around 25% abv while the second produces the high-strength 'heart' which is later reduced to, typically, 40% abv (80% US proof).

In the United States, applejack is lighter in character than calvados because it may be merged with up to 80% neutral spirit, although in practice the proportions are closer to 50/50. Such a product must be labelled 'Blended'.

As with all other American brandies, ageing must be for a minimum of two years, in oak wood containers, size unspecified.

Bonny Doon – a grappa and a 'Golden' Eau-de-vie

## LISTINGS

### Bonny Doon

This is one of the first fully-formed eaux-de-vie to emerge from Randall Grahm's fascinating experimental programme at Bonny Doon (see grappa section). The brandy is made from Golden Delicious apples and shows fine fruit aroma and good concentration of fruit characteristics in the flavour.

### Label

Bonny Doon Pomme Golden Apple Brandy.

### POMME GOLDEN APPLE BRANDY

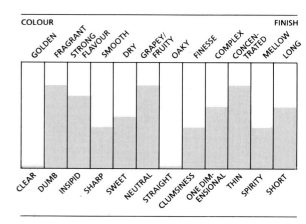

| COLOUR | | | | | | | | | | | | FINISH |
|--------|--|--|--|--|--|--|--|--|--|--|--|--------|
| GOLDEN | FRAGRANT | STRONG FLAVOUR | SMOOTH | DRY | GRAPEY/ FRUITY | OAKY | FINESSE | COMPLEX | CONCEN-TRATED | MELLOW | LONG | |
| CLEAR | DUMB | INSIPID | SHARP | SWEET | NEUTRAL | STRAIGHT | CLUMSINESS | ONE DIM-ENSIONAL | THIN | SPIRITY | SHORT | |

### Clear Creek

This is one of the fruit eaux-de-vie produced by an artisanal distillery in Portland, Oregon (see US grappa section). Broadly speaking, the apple brandy is like calvados (q.v.) from France, but there are some differences.

The distiller, Stephen McCarthy, combines the techniques used to make oak-aged calvados in Normandy and the Swiss/German spirit, Apfel-brand, which is distilled from a fermented mash of the whole fruit and is not aged. His brandy is said to have startlingly vivid apple flavour and aroma unlike anything from Calvados.

*Label*
Clear Creek Apple Brandy.

## CLEAR CREEK APPLE BRANDY

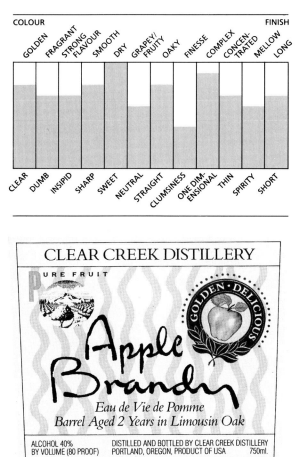

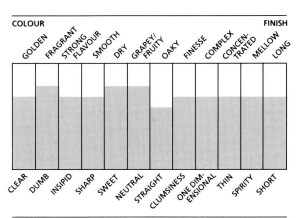

CLEAR CREEK DISTILLERY
PURE FRUIT
GOLDEN DELICIOUS
*Apple Brandy*
*Eau de Vie de Pomme*
*Barrel Aged 2 Years in Limousin Oak*

ALCOHOL 40% BY VOLUME (80 PROOF) — DISTILLED AND BOTTLED BY CLEAR CREEK DISTILLERY PORTLAND, OREGON, PRODUCT OF USA 750ml.

*The McCarthy Brothers grow and pick the fruit for their Apple Brandy Eau-de-vie de Pomme.*

## Laird

The applejack brandy is made from whole, tree-ripened apples such as Sweet Cider, Golden and Red Delicious, Jonathan, Pippin and, the very best, Wine Sap. The orchards are in the Delaware Valley. The cider is fermented naturally in 20 000-gallon oak vats, and there are no additives. This takes from 7 to 30 days immediately after the vintage, when it reaches about 12% abv strength.

The cider is double-distilled in pot-stills, the complete process taking several weeks to complete. As elsewhere, the entire distillation is carried out at the same time, once a year. The spirit is reduced to 65% abv for ageing, which takes place in 50-gallon charred-oak barrels for from four to eight years.

The firm is located in Scobeyville, New Jersey, and effectively comprises the entire applejack sector in the United States. The only other existing brand, Captain Applejack, better-known in the southern states, also belongs to Laird. The main sales areas are in the northern United States, but demand has been growing in Florida owing to the migration of northern applejack fans to the sunshine state.

Laird have been in existence since 1780 which makes them America's oldest brandy-distillers; the company is still family-run. They descend from Scottish immigrants who arrived in America in 1698, and brought with them distillation skills acquired through whisky-making in the Highlands.

*Labels*
Laird's Bonded 100% Proof 7½/10yo; Laird's Apple Brandy; Laird's Blended Applejack (35% apple brandy + 65% corn spirit).

## LAIRD APPLE BRANDY

# AUSTRALIA

Brandy-making in Australia began as a direct result of the mix of nationalities that landed on her soil, seeking to acquire some land and set up new lives for themselves. Many were French, German and Italian and the Australian climate was well-suited to growing vines, so the newcomers continued their practice of making light table wines to drink with their meals.

The northern Europeans who arrived to become new Australians – particularly the Dutch and the British – were, however, more accustomed to port and sherry, famous sweet fortified wines which traditionally were drunk either side of a meal. When some wine-makers eventually looked beyond the family table and began to produce on a commercial scale, they had to give some thought to the styles of wine that would be in demand.

To interest the British immigrants, it made sense to offer a choice of fortified wines but, in order to make them, wine spirit had to be distilled to fortify the base wines. Consequently, in addition to the vineyards that were in full production in the south of the country, distilleries were also established. Demand steadily grew and from 1901 there were detailed regulations covering the making and maturation of Australian brandy.

## GRAPE BRANDY

The regulations relating to the production of brandy in Australia, introduced at the turn of the century, did nothing at first to boost sales against imported brandies, which were mainly cognac. In 1907 the 2¼ million litres consumed divided evenly between home and European origin, but cognac's post-phylloxera recovery led to its taking a 75% share of the Australian market.

Cognac's scarcity during the First World War dropped it below half-share just as hostilities ended, and it continued to dwindle for the next ten years. In 1930–31, consumption of both home and imported brandies plummeted, but over the next 15 years home brandy sales built up again to record levels while imported spirits fell through the floor.

*The Australian climate and soil are well suited to growing vines.*

*Many of the Australian vineyards are located in flat alluvial fields.*

Consumption of home brandy rose steadily throughout the Second World War, doubling in the ten years to 1945. Cognac trickled back as supplies became available again, but it was the late 1960s before its share of the Australian market got back into double figures.

During the 1980s home brandy has been very successful, holding three-quarters of a market which has doubled in volume since the end of the Second World War.

There are modest exports in bottle, chiefly to Canada and a little to Japan.

Brandies from Greece, Cyprus, Italy and Spain are imported in bottle in sufficient quantities to give them a presence in the shops, and thus widen the choice available to the curious.

### The countryside

The geography of brandy-production in Australia, as in all non-specialist production areas of the world, is that of the wine industry – particularly where fortified wines and, hence, brandy are produced.

South Australia is called the 'Wine State' due to

the endless vineyards that stretch across the flat flood plains of the Murray River, but it is also famous for opal-mining, Grand Prix motor-racing and seafood. The Flinders Ranges act as an 800-km (497-mile) garden fence on to the outback which stretches away to the north, and along the coast beaches and fishing ports alternate with wild cliffs and rock formations.

Victoria is seen as the 'Garden State', an all-year-round visual treat with each season ushering in its particular colours as the profusion of fruit and flowers bud and flourish. History is still highly visible here, giving easy access to traces of the tall ships, the gold-rush days and the early explorers.

You pass from forest to wheatland, and then to desert if you travel far enough, and a speciality of the countryside is the ghost-towns left forlornly when the gold ran out. In summer, though, life is lived at the coast in boats, on water skis and on jetties, from which the fishing is good.

New South Wales is the oldest of the six states in Australia and the temperatures there are less extreme because it lies within the temperate climate zone. Bushland, mountain ranges, lush valley floors where the rivers meander and the roads go dead straight, vineyards and national parks the size of English counties are all to be found here, and you begin to understand what people mean when they claim that New South Wales has everything that the rest of Australia has, but much closer together.

Riverina District on the Murrumbidgee River, where brandy is produced, lies west of the Great Dividing Range. It is mainly flat, alluvial land with scarcely perceptible ripples of height variation. Temperatures are often very high – over 40C – and, since rainfall is inadequate, river water reaches it by irrigation.

## History

The first grapes to become established in Australia were the Muscat Gordo Blanco and the Doradillo. When the seedless Sultana was introduced to the Murray River overproduction became quite common and distillation was often the only course open to growers.

The early distillation vessels in Australia were pot-stills, which gave the more creative distillers the opportunity to develop something a little more interesting than straight, characterless grape spirit, so, in parallel, brandy styles started to evolve. However, pot-stills were an expensive and tedious means of obtaining the highly-refined neutral spirit that was increasingly needed. Rectifying plates had to be added for this operation and the spirit produced in separate batches, having to be recharged after each distillation run.

Consequently, it was not long before continuous stills based on Coffey's design were brought over from Europe to do the job in a more logical way. The first of those went to Renmark and the Barossa Valley, both in South Australia.

*The Australian brandy market has doubled since WW II.*

In 1901, the Distillation Act laid down regulations covering the making and maturation of brandy in Australia, both to ensure the purity of the product and protect the revenue of the excise department. By the 1920s, brandy-making was well-established in the Barossa, Southern Vales, Renmark and Berri areas of South Australia, and near Mildura in Victoria further east. Today, Waikere and Loxton (South Australia) and Griffith in New South Wales have gained distilleries, and together these locations constitute the main Australian brandy-making centres.

## The brandy

Australian brandy is varied in character from the light mixing styles to the fuller, more pronounced sipping styles, with most stages in between according to the combination of pot- and continuous still spirits used in each brand's blend. An extra element of fruit nuance often occurs from the use of various 'enhancement' flavourings (see below).

## Grapes

The grapes widely grown today for making Australian brandy still include the Doradillo and Sultana that were used in the early days. Newer varieties in use are the Pedro Ximenez and the Palomino, famous in Spanish sherry production, and the Trebbiano which is found all over Italy. This latter grape, which, of course, is also known as the Ugni Blanc, is sometimes called the White Hermitage in Australia.

These are all white grapes and they are chosen for their pronounced acidity and their lack of marked varietal flavours. Such grapes translate well into brandy. Gently-pressed 'free-run juice' is fermented at a low temperature in order to retain the more delicate aromatics in the grapes.

The resulting wine is not distilled on its lees as is often done in European brandy-making, but is left turbid so as to contribute some extra flavour elements if it is to be distilled in a pot-still.

Apart from caramel and sugar, which, in tiny amounts, are permitted contents in brandies all over the world, Australian brandy may also have grape juice (or concentrate), wine, prune juice, honey and 'flavourings' added to it.

## Distillation

Pot-stills were the first type to be used in Australia and there was a local version that was cleverly designed to adapt to a continuous function when needed by means of removable rectification plates

127

*In the foreground is part of the 1200-acre vineyard owned by Angove near the Murray River, South Australia.*

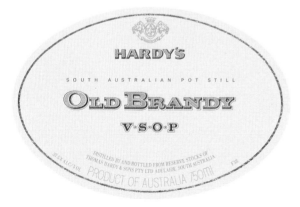

in the column. Apart from that, the traditional Australian pot-still has a highly distinctive appearance with a cylindrical pot and fully upright column.

At the top of the column is a water vessel through which the vapour pipe passes, and it acts an intermediate or auxiliary cooler before the cooling coil proper over the condenser. It was designed by a South Australian coppersmith called Bergstrom, whose prototype was installed at the Horndale distillery south of Adelaide in the 1890s.

Several wine-distillations – Cognac's *brouillis* – usually have to be carried out in order to have a fill for each second and final brandy-distillation, the *bonne chauffe*. The still has to be thoroughly cleaned out for this operation, and it was to avoid this repetitive and laborious task that whisky-distillers in Scotland began to build stills in pairs;

the wash (first run) and spirit (second run) stills each had a single function.

Continuous stills may also be used to make Australian brandy and there are many designs, all stemming from Coffey's famous model, in use in the industry today. Blair, Engelbrett, Jennings and Whitehill are some of the variations found in the distilleries.

To avoid excessive ceiling heights, the long column is usually broken into two or three sections. Spirit collected from the very top of a continuous still is neutral and very high in strength, so an intermediate point must be chosen for drawing off the brandy spirit so that it is below the 83% legal maximum.

With a continuous still, the brandy-maker cannot choose a 'heart' or 'middle cut' as is done with a pot-still; all he can do is opt for a certain strength at which to tap, and he has to accept the 'package' of congenerics and flavour elements that go with it. Australian brandy comes off the still between 74% and 83% abv.

## Maturation

Australian brandy is reduced in strength by about a quarter before it starts its maturation in wood. Pure, filtered water takes it down to around 60% abv, which is an optimum level for the oak

A section of the brandy bond store, Mildara Wines, Marbein, Victoria.

environment it is about to enter. Spirit above 60% tends to 'denature' the wood and remove elasticity, while anything much lower would mean mere water, not brandy, was being aged.

Regulations require a minimum of two years in oak, but there is a very wide choice left to the maker to decide his house-style since the vessels may be anything from 300 litres to 45000 litres in capacity.

If oaky aromas and flavours are wanted, smaller casks will be used since they put more surface area in contact with the brandy, and relatively fresh wood will have more vanillin and tannins to impart. Evaporation rates in Australia's climate cost about 2–3% volume-loss each year, and, of course, the process also gradually reduces the alcoholic strength.

Batches of brandy are classified by style and quality and stipulated quantities may be blended or kept separate, according to their eventual role, prior to beginning ageing. They receive an official 'birthday' – the start-point of their maturation period – when they are put into wood. The lighter brandies will not be left to age much beyond the two-year minimum, but the spirits with fuller flavour and more complexity – usually pot-still products – will age for up to 20 years.

With ageing complete, final blending to house style is carried out and the alcohol level again reduced with pure water; 37% abv is the customary bottling strength in Australia. Total stocks of Australian brandy maturing at any given time are maintained at about four times the draw-off rate.

The still room at Château Reynella – Hardy's three pot-stills produce 80 000 litres of spirit a day.

## Label information

Two distinct styles of Australian brandy are marketed – one to take as a long drink with mixers, the other to sip and enjoy for its own taste and character. The mixing style is widely used as the base for a range of add-in flavours, rather as vodka is used elsewhere, and the brandy itself has a wide range of input from light to quite full-flavoured. The lighter brandies contain a greater proportion of highly-refined spirit, but at least 25% of any Australian brandy must be distilled at or under the legal stipulation of 83% abv.

The sipping style is aged longer and has more to offer in aroma, resonance, complexity and length. It is more expensive, house-styles vary in detail and you appraise this type of brandy as you would a fine spirit from Jerez or Armagnac.

*A brandy's age is usually that of the youngest spirit in the blend. For St. Agnes, 'very old' means 10 years minimum.*

If it is Australian brandy, it will say so on the label in 3 mm type-size. 'Bottled in Australia' means the brandy, including cognac, was imported in bulk; otherwise the name of the country may only be used on a label if the contents are wholly produced or made there. The words 'cognac' and 'armagnac' may not be used to indicate a type or style of brandy; if either word appears on the label, that is what is inside the bottle. Such protection is automatically part of the national law in member-states of the European Community, but is a matter of negotiation in other countries.

'Matured' applies only to brandy aged for a minimum of two years in wood; 'Old' indicates minimum five years' wood-ageing; and 'Very Old' means minimum ten years in wood. When brandy is released into sale from the excise department, a certificate of age accompanies it. 'Australian Blended Brandy' is a mix of pot- and continuous still spirits.

## Places to visit

South Australia's Murray River is the continent's mightiest watercourse, 2450 km (1522 miles) long and stretching tributary fingers into New South Wales and Victoria, the two other states where brandy-making is important. Loxton and Waikerie, well-known as distilling towns, are also important as centres of the citrus fruit industry. Paddle-wheel steamers used to be the main means of transport to the coast, and now they are used for pleasure cruises. It is a very peaceful environment and Renmark, one of the distilling/wine towns, is where Australia's first irrigation system was set up.

The Mount Lofty Ranges, a half-hour out from Adelaide, are good for scenic drives and picnics, and the Torrens Gorge, in the Adelaide Hills, is arresting. In the same location is Hahndorf, essentially still a German immigrants' town, where the shops sell fine craftwork – and food – made in their old traditions.

The Barossa Valley, too, was first settled by German immigrants in the early 1800s, and much of its 19th-century charm remains. Most of the vineyards welcome visitors and there are special cycle tracks for those interested in doing a cycling tour of the wineries. Nuriootpa town took shape in the 1840s as a stopover for travellers en route to, or from, the copper mines at Burra, itself worth a visit.

There are many national parks in the state and there is one at the tip of two of the three peninsulas near Adelaide. Emus, kangaroos, koalas, possums and penguins are among the wildlife on Kangaroo Island, whose western end is also a national park. Eyre Peninsula has wonderful surf and quite superb scenery, and some of the scenes from *Jaws* were filmed on this coast.

The Flinders Ranges are wild country with spectacular gorges and impossible waterfalls; there is very good, but demanding, trail-walking throughout. These were once Aborigine tribal lands and there are rock paintings and carvings to be seen. One of the gorges opens out to the fantastic Wilpena Pound, an enormous mountain-girt amphitheatre once used to hide rustled livestock.

It is a long way from Adelaide to the opal-mining area at Coober Pedy – 900 km (559 miles) – but the scale of Australia is such that you tend to accept travelling greater distances. Opals were first mined here in the 1920s and, to escape the heat, the people live, as well as work, underground. The name means 'white man's hole in the ground' in

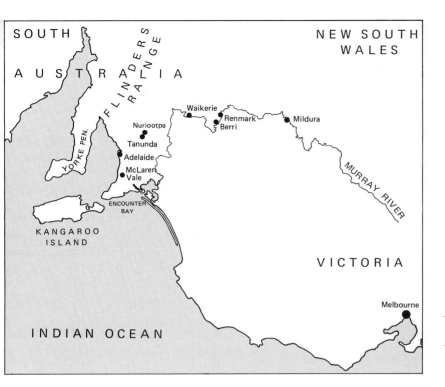

*Most Australian brandy-producers are found on the flood plains of the Murray River, where distillation was first introduced to remedy overproduction of the sultana grapes.*

Aboriginal dialect, and there is even an underground church.

Further north is Oodnadatta, where the main road also serves as the cricket square, and to the east lies Lake Eyre, the salt pan where Donald Campbell set his world land speed record in 1954. West of Coober Pedy is an interesting area where visitors are not welcome – the prohibited area of Woomera where the rocket ranges used to be. It is an empty quarter, however, and is the start of the Great Victoria Desert.

Running west across the territory is the trans-Australia railway which is the world's longest straight railway line. Just over the state border in Western Australia, off the coast highway, is what used to be the township of Eucla. People had to move out of their houses years ago when the desert sands began to encroach, and today it lies completely buried.

Victoria has 30 national parks, snow-covered mountains, plains of wheat crops and a dramatically variegated coastline, which alternates between long, sandy beaches and rough-hewn cliffs and headlands. There are a hundred wineries to visit, and the brandy country in the state's north-west is a continuation of the South Australia stretch on the same Murray River, this time with Mildura township as the fulcrum of the industry. It has been transformed into an outback oasis by irrigation of the Murray, and olives, oranges and avocados also grow throughout the district. Further upriver, the pioneer settlements at Swan Hill and Echuca recreate the townships as they were in the paddlewheel steamer era.

Victoria is compact and a glance will show its map to be much 'busier' and more concentrated. The best coastal scenery lies along the Great Ocean Road running west, with the Twelve Apostles rock pillar group, the natural archway of London Bridge and the Loch Ard gorge in the Port Campbell national park. At the end of the highway is the historic town of Portland, where the first permanent settlement in Victoria was built in 1834, and you can visit the home of the first pioneer family.

Surface gold was discovered in 1851 west of Melbourne and the townships of Bendigo and Ballarat grew as a result of the huge numbers of prospectors who teemed into the area. A famous nugget found there weighed over 86 kg (189 lb), and Sovereign Hill recreates the goldrush atmosphere for today's visitors. You can pan for gold, ride in the old Cobb and Co. coach and stay overnight at the Government Camp. The Eureka Stockade, where the miners rebelled against the government in 1854, is still there, and nearby is a gold museum.

Mount Buffalo is an uplifted plateau with steep cliffs from which the surrounding countryside may be surveyed, as if from an aircraft. It is a national park in the Great Dividing Range where the alpine

*Stalwarts like Errol Richard Jubilee Gates, underpinned the success of the Australian brandy industry.*

reaches are ski pistes in the winter and wonderful bush-walking and horse-trekking trails in the summer.

East Gippsland, in the south-east, has a Mediterranean quality to its climate and it is known as the Victorian Riviera.

Tiny penguins *en masse* shuffle up a beach on Phillip Island each day after feeding. It looks like the end of the late shift at a factory – in a way that is exactly what it is – and it is a delightful spectacle as they trudge straight to their nests.

In Melbourne, you can eat dinner on the move in, of all things, a tramcar, and there are several theatre-restaurants where you can eat and watch a show at the same time. There is a wide range of ethnic cuisine to be found; the aromas of Turkish, Chinese, Vietnamese, Italian and Greek dishes, among others, reach out from the restaurants as you stroll past.

You can visit Old Melbourne Gaol where Ned Kelly was hanged in 1880 and walk through Captain Cook's family cottage, which was brought out brick by brick from Yorkshire in England and re-erected in Fitzroy Gardens. Other houses you should visit are Como, in lovely colonial style at South Yarra, and Rippon Lea, a mansion in spectacular gardens at Elsternwick.

# LISTINGS

## Angove

St. Agnes Old has an average age of 10–12 years but there is very old spirit in the blend of up to 40 years of age to add depth of flavour. The age of the brandy has to be defined by that of the youngest spirit in the blend. 'Old' means a minimum of five years' oak-ageing and 'Very Old' means a minimum 10 years'.

St. Agnes is the patron saint of purity, hence Angove's use of her name for their brand of clean and unsullied spirit that is double-distilled from pot-stills. Most of the small hogshead oak casks host their brandies for from 2 to 20 years; after blending, the final spirit spends further time in oak to 'marry'.

St. Agnes is distilled from wine made from White Hermitage, Semillon, Doradillo, Pedro and Sultana grapes; the proportions are a secret. Not every country allows wine and spirit to be produced from the same location, but in Australia it is possible for the whole integral process to take shape unhindered under the same roof. This is the system used at Angove.

Angove was begun in 1886 by an immigrant doctor from Cornwall in Britain. Dr. W. T. Angove, MRCS, planted vines and vintaged wines at Tea Tree Gully, where he had set up his country practice. Later his sons moved to Renmark and in 1910 built the first winery and distillery on the River Murray. It was here that the first St. Agnes brandy was produced.

Angove wines and brandies were a way of life for generations of the family and those who worked for them. There are instances of men totalling 60 years of service in the business and many remember the family dog called, of course, Brandy.

The Angoves were resourceful and innovative and it was they who invented the 'bag-in-box' wine-pack in 1965, a concept which has been adopted all over the world. There was also room for a sense of humour, too, in their marketing, as with Château Downunda wine that became so popular abroad.

Visitors welcome without appointment. The museum and tourist information centre at Tea Tree Gully are located in what was the original winery.

## Labels

St. Agnes *** 2/5yo; St. Agnes Old 7/40yo; St. Agnes Very Old 14/40yo.

*St. Agnes, distilled from White Hermitage, Semillon, Doradillo Pedro and Sultana grapes.*

## ST. AGNES OLD

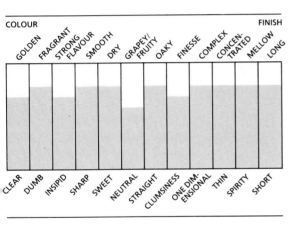

### Berri Estates

This company began producing brandy from surplus raisins and sultanas from the 1918 Riverland harvest. Fruit-production greatly increased as veterans from the Great War settled the district and in 1922 the distillation capacity was expanded under the aegis of the newly-formed Berri Growers Co-operative. Today the group are the largest wine-producers in Australia and their winery at Glossop, South Australia, is the largest in the country.

Visitors are welcome.

### Labels

Brandy 3yo; 60th Anniversary.

### Château Yaldara

Château Yaldara's owner, Hermann Thumm, developed a revolutionary vacuum distillation method which imparts more grape flavour to the distillate. The brandies are young but generous in style; they are vintaged two or three years back from the year that they go on sale.

Château Yaldara is a spectacular grouping of stone buildings at Lyndoch in South Australia's Barossa Valley. They were resurrected from the ruins of an old flour mill by Thumm, who arrived from Germany in the 1940s. There is even a battlemented tower that would look positively Gothic if it were not for the gloom-chasing Australian sunshine. Gardens and lakes surround the complex which includes the distillery that was built in 1974. They have about 35 hectares under vine.

Visitors are welcome by appointment. There are daily tours of the château, a film on the wine-making and a garden bistro open daily for lunch.

### Label

Vintage Brandy 2/4yo.

### Hardy

The distillation wines for Hardy's brandies are made at the Cyrilton winery at Waikerie. Three pot-stills produce 80 000 litres of spirit a day which is then transported to McLaren Vale, where it is put into small oak casks.

Most of the brandy matures for two-to-three years, although some is left for longer periods to feed the stocks of older brandies used for the VSOP.

There is a cooperage at McLaren Vale which turns out 400 new French oak hogsheads and puncheons each year, mainly for wines.

*Hardy's headquarters at McLaren Vale – most of the brandy matures for two to three years.*

Thomas Hardy could well have felt daunted by the name of the spot where he landed from Devon, in Britain, in 1850—Port Misery. However, he tackled a number of ways of making his fortune, including gold-prospecting and cattle-driving. In 1853 he bought a property on the River Torrens and planted vines.

Over the four years that it took for the vines to begin producing fruit he tended his fields and dug a cellar in preparation for the wine he was to make in 1857. His progress in marketing wines, and later brandy, was steady from that point onwards. His wines won gold medals in Bordeaux and Paris, and he was exporting to Britain by 1859. There is a statue to him in McLaren Vale town. The present head of the company, Sir James Hardy, was a skipper in the Americas Cup yacht races.

Although Thomas Hardy had aspirations to make a 'pure brandy equal to the best brands of cognac', the still house in 1886 was small and modestly equipped. The first still had been an old Cornish boiler with a column fixed to the top, and the next was a 700-gallon jarrah vat with the column similarly attached.

The Black Bottle brandy is unusual by its being distilled twice—once through a continuous still and once through a pot-still. Very unorthodox, possibly unique, but it yields a very smooth three-year-old brandy after maturation in oak casks. The VSOP is wholly pot-still brandy from Doradillo grapes picked early to enhance acidity levels. The spirit matures for at least 25 years, making it one of the world's most mature VSOPs surely. It has won a number of awards.

### Labels
Black Bottle 3yo; Old Brandy VSOP 25yo

### HARDY BLACK BOTTLE

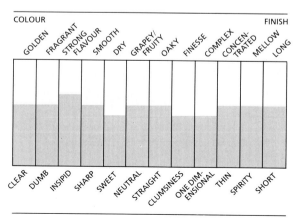

### HARDY'S OLD BRANDY VSOP

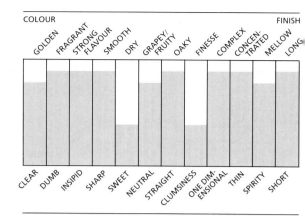

### Penfolds/Stock

One of the biggest names in Australian and New Zealand wines and spirits production makes brandy under licence at Nuriootpa, South Australia, in the style of the Italian firm, Stock (q.v.).

The brandy is a light, approachable spirit, made from Doradillo and Pedro Ximénez grapes (the latter one of Spain's renowned Sherry vines). It is distilled from both pot- and Coffey (continuous) stills and averages eight years' maturation in American oak hogsheads.

### Label
Stock 84 8yo.

### PENFOLDS STOCK 84

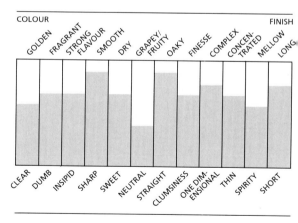

### Renmano

A company that began in 1916 as a co-operative effort by 130 grape-growers at Riverland. They bought the distillery of Château Tanunda and produced spirit for a number of years before going over to fortified wines and, latterly, table wines.

Today Renmano is part of the very large Berri Consolidated Co-operatives concern and calls on production from over 3000 hectares of vineyards. Visitors to Renmark are welcome by appointment.

### Label
*** Brandy.

### Roseworthy

This is the renowned agricultural college 50 km north of Adelaide that produces the gifted winemakers and viticulturalists now making top-class wines and brandies all over the world. It was founded in 1883 and its 'vineyard of the world' contains just about every known grape variety. They have five hectares under vine but grapes for their commercial production are bought in from the best grape-growing areas.

Visitors welcome by appointment; there is a college farm and museum in addition to tours around the campus itself.

### Label
Liqueur Brandy 8/10yo.

### Seppelt

The house-style is soft and aromatic with fair dryness and good fruit presence. There is a sniff of wood there but the overall feel is of lightness and approachability.

When Joseph Seppelt arrived in Australia in 1851 he planted a wide range of crops and established cattle on his land. There had to be an element of make-do and his first wine was made in the dairy shed. In 1867, the Seppelts built Seppeltsfield, a winery complex in turreted stone, and very grand in appearance.

Château Tanunda is also a splendid stone construction. It was built in 1890 and concentrated on brandy-production throughout the early 1900s, before it was acquired by Seppelt. Consequently, when Seppelt bought the château in 1916, large stocks of older brandy came with it.

The turreting theme was continued, and today even the storage tanks are finished in this way to conform with the original buildings. The family mausoleum on a hill lends quite a dynastic touch to the estate. An interesting feature of the company's Great Western winery are the six kilometres of underground tunnels, dug by goldminers in the 1860s, for storing wines at cool and constant temperatures.

*The Seppelt family had been producing wine for nearly half a century before they acquired Château Tanunda with its large stocks of old brandy.*

### Label
Château Tanunda 3yo.

### CHÂTEAU TANUNDA

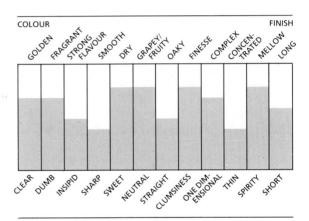

# AROUND THE WORLD

Mercifully, there is that streak in human nature that encourages creative people to forge ahead with an idea whether or not there is any local, cultural or historical precedent for it. Throughout the wine and brandy world there are countless instances of innovators who have broken the rules to produce better than the rules will allow.

This short chapter highlights some individual brandies which you could encounter anywhere on your travels that interesting drinks are on sale because lines of communication between like-minded people have a way of being formed. There are also some that are so omnipresent in their home markets that they must be acknowledged.

Quality comes from individual attitude and effort, not from national legislation or long tradition – although they can help. Good quality can emerge anywhere whether or not there is a context of tradition. In Germany, for example, there was never any wine left over to make brandy so the Germans imported it; in England a cider-maker strove for ten years to overturn a 200-year-old ban on brandy-making; Armenian producers decided to make better use of a 'national treasure' that otherwise served only the party fat cats.

These listings are by brand name, which is only sometimes the same as the name of the company.

## ARMENIA

Today, along the line of Asia's ancient Silk Road, nomads still distil spirit by catching drips that condense against a bowl of cold water suspended over a boiling pan of fermented beer. In parallel, however, the Ararat distillery at troubled Yerevan in Armenia has for over a century been producing fine spirit by more widely-recognized methods.

During those 100 years, an extraordinary range of old brandies, called the 'Golden Reserve' – among the world's oldest old-brandy stores – has accrued in the distillery's cellars, which are scooped out of Mount Ararat. Casks of these

*German wines are no longer used to produce Weinbrand, though the practice of making brandy in Germany almost certainly predates its development in the Cognac area.*

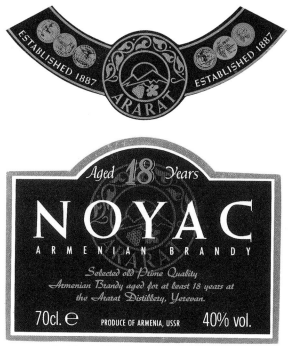

A Noyac double-distilled brandy – aged for 18 years in Armenian oak.

Armenian brandies are now being sent to the West for bottling and sale in the interests of gaining hard currency – which was also the reason for recent auctions of very old wines from the Russian czar's cellars.

The offer was made off the cuff to Varta Ouzounian, an expatriate Armenian now based in London, who went out to Armenia to help in the relief work after the recent earthquake there. To date the brandy had only been served at state banquets in Russia, although Sir Winston Churchill is said to have been enthusiastic about it when it was on tap to all of the national leaders at the Yalta conference in 1945.

The strength of the distillate is measured in similar ways throughout the world.

## Noyac

There are three very old brandies in this range that utilizes those impressive mature stocks: a ten-year-old, an 18-year-old and a 25-year-old. They are all double-distilled in traditional pot-stills from local grapes and bottled at 40% abv.

They are richly mellow in style with a pleasant toasted tang which may come from the charring degree of the Armenian oak they are aged in and the extraordinary 80° temperature range – from –30°C in winter to 50°C in summer – they experience when withdrawn from the protection of the Mount Ararat cellars.

The name of the brandy stems from the spring water used in distillation of the spirit and the tradition that Noah's ark came to rest on Mount Ararat: Noyac means 'the spring of Noah'.

### NOYAC 10 YEARS-OLD

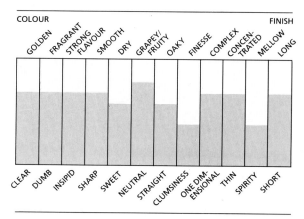

### NOYAC 18 YEARS-OLD

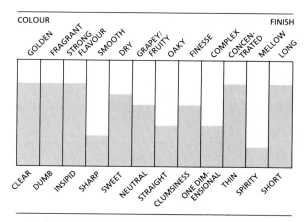

## NOYAC 25 YEARS-OLD

| COLOUR | | | | | | | | | | | | FINISH |
|--------|--|--|--|--|--|--|--|--|--|--|--|--------|
| GOLDEN | FRAGRANT | STRONG FLAVOUR | SMOOTH | DRY | GRAPEY/ FRUITY | OAKY | FINESSE | COMPLEX | CONCEN-TRATED | MELLOW | LONG | |
| CLEAR | DUMB | INSIPID | SHARP | SWEET | NEUTRAL | STRAIGHT | CLUMSINESS | ONE DIM-ENSIONAL | THIN | SPIRITY | SHORT | |

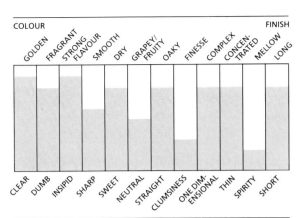

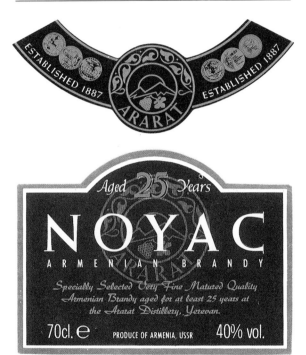

*The name Noyac means 'spring of Noah'.*

# CYPRUS

The island has a well-documented history of wine cultivation and distillation that goes back almost 800 years. The production companies have formed their brandy blends with an eye to both the expectations of visiting foreigners and their own traditions. The latter include the drinking of low-strength 'brandies' (less than 30% abv) as an alternative to wine with meals, usually in the tavernas.

Cypriot brandies are smooth and gentle, with high-strength distillation removing spirity harshness even before they are reduced with water.

*In all grape brandy producing countries, distillers mature brandy in wood to develop its potential.*

Walnut and fruit peel extracts are added for flavour. Brandy is practically the Cypriots' national drink and the majority of those available are full 40% abv strength. All brandies age for a minimum of three years.

### Adonis

This is a carefully-produced brandy, dubbed VSOP, which comes out rather well in the face of the initial scepticism of those who encounter it. It is aged for around 15 years in Limousin oak and has a delicate, lightly-wooded persona. It is sold in a square-section decanter.

Also from the same firm is Sodap, also VSOP and also over 15 years-old, but with a grapier, more affirmative character. This sells in a regularly-shaped bottle which holds only 66 cl as against 75 cl in the decanter.

These brandies are from the Sodap company which also produce Commandaria, the celebrated dessert wine of the Knights Templar crusaders, made on Cyprus since the 12th century.

## SODAP ADONIS VSOP

| COLOUR | | | | | | | | | | | | FINISH |
|--------|--|--|--|--|--|--|--|--|--|--|--|--------|
| GOLDEN | FRAGRANT | STRONG FLAVOUR | SMOOTH | DRY | GRAPEY/ FRUITY | OAKY | FINESSE | COMPLEX | CONCEN-TRATED | MELLOW | LONG | |
| CLEAR | DUMB | INSIPID | SHARP | SWEET | NEUTRAL | STRAIGHT | CLUMSINESS | ONE DIM-ENSIONAL | THIN | SPIRITY | SHORT | |

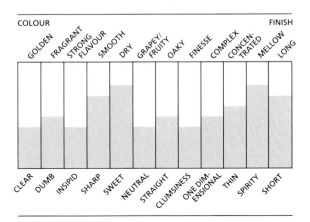

*Adonis is aged for 15 years in Limousin oak.*

## SODAP VSOP

| COLOUR | | | | | | | | | | | | FINISH |
|---|---|---|---|---|---|---|---|---|---|---|---|---|
| GOLDEN | FRAGRANT | STRONG FLAVOUR | SMOOTH | DRY | GRAPEY/ FRUITY | OAKY | FINESSE | COMPLEX | CONCEN- TRATED | MELLOW | LONG | |
| CLEAR | DUMB | INSIPID | SHARP | SWEET | NEUTRAL | STRAIGHT | CLUMSINESS | ONE DIM- ENSIONAL | THIN | SPIRITY | SHORT | |

### Anglias

This is the brand name of Haggipavlu which covers a range of at least seven different brandies. Starting at the top end there is a decanter pack, a 1919 VO, a 15-year-old Alexander, a five-year-old Antica, a Red Label, a standard and a one-star standard. This latter description goes back to the days in Cyprus when more stars on a label meant better quality; the sequence was one-star, two-stars, three-stars and VO. Anglias is the best-selling brand on the

island. The company also does a wine eau-de-vie with herbs called Grapal.

Haggipavlu was founded in 1844 in Limassol and was the first firm to produce brandy on Cyprus. That was in 1872 after a still was brought in from Marseilles in France, and brandy became so popular that the company came close to giving up wine-production to concentrate solely on distillation.

In 1914, at the International Exhibition in London, the company's brandy shared the gold medal in the brandy competition with the Napoleon cognac from Bisquit. Its house style must suit British tastes because the brand name originates from the blend that was exported to the UK long before becoming available on the island.

### Master's XO

A 12-year-old Limousin-aged brandy from Palomino grapes made in locally-crafted pot-stills, and sufficiently well-regarded by its proprietors to make further information about it confidential. A companion brand is VO 43, one of the very low-strength Cypriot 'brandies' which is, nonetheless, aged for three years. This one is claimed to be distilled to 96% abv by pot-still, which must make

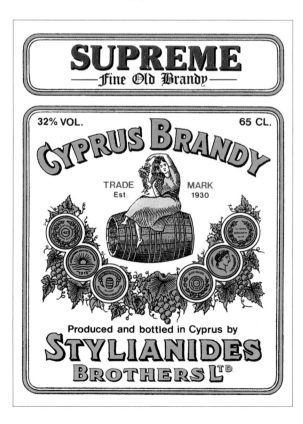

*Brandy-makers worldwide who aspire to a cognac-style spirit follow similar methods.*

it the world's most efficient unit of this type. Or perhaps they distil three times.

Other Cypriot brands are Stylianides Supreme and Keo.

## GERMANY

Distilling has had a long and learned tradition in the territories that are still coalescing into today's Germany. The seal of the German Wine Distillers Federation shows that the first such body goes back to 1588. From the monks who first distilled herbal and fruit potions, through the medieval surgeon-barbers who enjoyed the monopoly of alcohol manufacture and dispensation, Germans have utilized distillation to the full.

However, as in other north European countries, the emphasis has been on distillation of cereals to produce a wide range of the famous schnapps spirits. German vineyards lie on the northern limits for grape-production and vines have had to compete with cereal crops for land-space; some vineyard slopes were so steep that the workers often had to be tied on to prevent their falling over the edges. The limited production available meant that all the grapes were used for wine-making, and supplies for making brandy had to be brought in from elsewhere.

Today, most German brandy is made from semi-fortified wines – *vins vinés* – brought in from France and Italy. This has led to something of a lack of identity for brandies produced in Germany, although they are all well-made to high standards.

Apart from the distilleries, there is no point of origin, no 'birthplace' within the country to furnish a national image for German brandy, so in name, at least, it is a little anonymous. The only means of forming impressions is through the brands themselves; the best-sellers are straightforwardly German in persona, but some brands are French in presentation, and, indeed, in origin.

*Weinbrand*, the German word for grape brandy, was coined in 1907 by Hugo Asbach to describe his own product. It was officially adopted in 1971 to designate grape brandy made in Germany. Standard weinbrand must age for six months in oak and *Uralt* or *Alter* means a brandy that has had at least a year's ageing.

Production of weinbrand is just over nine million cases a year. Each batch of distillate is numbered and samples are held by the authorities for examination in the event of complaint. Recently, out of 18.5 million bottles sold, the Asbach company had just 30 complaints – and 25 of the bottles returned were empty!

There are several important firms producing good brandy.

### Asbach

The name that epitomizes German brandy and is well-distributed around the world. The Uralt they produce comes from Armagnac, Italian and Charente wine (some of it through the cognac company owned by the group) which is piped under the road from the station in Rüdesheim to the distillery. The brandy is a blend of pot- and continuous still spirit and is aged for over two years in small oak casks before fine-tuning in larger containers. A certain amount of new wood is bought each year for ageing new spirit.

The distillery was set up in 1892 by Hugo Asbach, who evolved the blend specifically for Anglo-Saxon palates. It meant putting more emphasis on taste and smoothness than on aroma as often applies with cognac. Asbach Uralt is a richer, rounder brandy than many cognacs and has good distribution – it is even available in the Falklands.

### ASBACH URALT

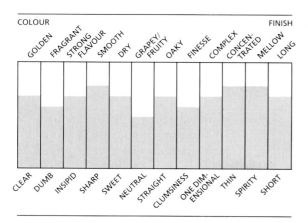

### Dujardin Fine

This is a cognac brandy in all but name. The wine derives from the Fins Bois zone of the Charentes in France, and is double-distilled in pot-stills in Germany. It then ages for eight years in small Limousin oak barrels. Also: Dujardin Imperial, ages minimum one year in Limousin oak; Melcher's Rat, light and mild.

Part of the Racke International company began in the 1600s when French forbears, then called Raquet, settled in the Rheingau and entered the wine trade. The other side of the company dates

*Carl Jung ages its brandies at Schloss Boosenberg for from 4½ to 30 years.*

from 1743 when Henricus Melcher set up as a 'chartered brandwein-distiller' in Urdingen. Dujardin was the name of the family in Cognac who supplied the Melchers with distilling wine and with whom a joint company was later formed.

### Goethe

The XO is made from German wine and ages for at least six years, although some of the blend is nearly 30-years-old. The VSOP is minimum 4½-years-old.

The Carl Jung firm has been established for a century and they mature their brandies in the very pretty Schloss Boosenberg (which may be visited) on the River Rhine at Rüdesheim. They have local vineyards (not for brandy-production) and are also in the slightly spoilsport business of alcohol-free wines.

### Mariacron

This is a light, smooth brandy that became the top seller in Europe in less than 20 years. It is made in continuous stills at the Mariacron monastery near Oppenheim, where the monks have distilled brandy since the tail-end of last century. It ages for up to a year in Limousin casks. Also: Chantre and Attaché brands.

The Eckes company dates from 1857 and had rapid success with their Chantre brandy after its introduction in 1953. The company acquired the Mariacron monastery in 1961 and it is from that date that the 'new' brand began its phenomenal growth, giving Eckes a second hit and underlining the popularity of the house-style.

### Scharlachberg Meisterbrand

This brandy is a big, friendly pussycat with full, soft flavour and a gentle 36% abv strength. It spends two years in Limousin oak but the barrels are three times larger than the traditional ageing casks so there is little woodiness in the blend. The wines come in from the Charentes.

The company dates from 1898 as a 'Cognac Distillery' in Bingen, but removed the French term in 1919 after agreements at Versailles. It is now owned by Seagram Germany, who took it over in 1987.

### SCHARLACHBERG MEISTERBRAND

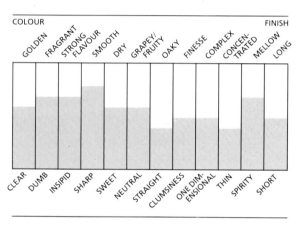

*In many rural areas, grape vintage time is a short but labour-intensive period which often involves every member of the family.*

# MEXICO

Any book on world brandy is more or less bound to include Mexico, if only to register the extraordinary popularity of the spirit there and to offer a momentary genuflection to the world's biggest brandy brand. The total market there is worth between 14 and 15 million cases, a remarkable volume that is out of all proportion to Mexico's modest wine-production figures.

The main grape-growing area is in Sonora State, where half of the country's vineyards are to be found. Most of the production from the half-dozen specialist crushing units there goes to brandy-making, and the majority grapes are Thomson Seedless and Perlette. Over 90% of the grapes grown throughout Mexico are used to make brandy, the gallonage of which is almost ten times greater than that of wine.

The brandy boom seems to have been triggered off after the last war when the French prevailed upon the Mexican government to ban the use of the word 'coñac' by the country's distillers. When the brand-owners opted for the English-language term 'brandy', the snob value attracted a lot of attention – and custom.

Curiously enough, it was in the Mexico of Cortés, as early as the 1530s, that the very first graftings of European vines on to native stock took place to protect against phylloxera. A quirk of Cortés' land-gift conditions to colonists was that 1000 vines had to be planted for every 100 Indians living and working on the property.

The broad style of Mexican brandies is very affable, but bland, in order to make them as adaptable as possible for straight drinking or mixing. Some serve in the way vodka does in other social settings – merely to supercharge the orange juice. When it comes to sipping styles, imported

*Wine presses employ a number of different means to achieve the same end.*

brands, principally from Spain but also from elsewhere in Europe and from North America, are staple. There are, however, a number of carefully made pot-still brandies produced in Mexico, often under the umbrella of a larger, high-volume operation.

The blandness of Mexican brandy comes mainly from the high-strength continuous distillation methods employed, but also from the Mission grapes that are still largely used. These are the vines that the Franciscan friars established in Mexico before taking them to plant in the vineyards of the 21 mission stations that they established between 1769 and 1823 in a chain running north into California. Parras, a valley 800 km (497 miles) north-west of Mexico City, may have been the original grape-cultivation centre in the Americas and several brandy-distillers operate in the area.

The commercial importance of brandy cannot sensibly be ignored by many of the more individualistic Mexican distillers, many of whom would otherwise just be making wine.

### Almacenes Guajardo

The company name of brandy-distillers who operate from the oldest winery on the American continent. The Vinícola del Marqués Aguayo was founded in 1593 at Parras by a Spanish army captain who came across groves of wild vines in a valley.

### Casa Madero

A distillery that produces fine brandy from pot-stills, and which has done so since 1870, when the dynamic young proprietor brought a still and installation engineers over from Cognac to get things started. A grandson fomented the 1910

revolution in Mexico and became the country's president. This is another of the very early wineries that were established in the area of Parras; the original unit on the Casa Madero site dates from 1626.

Visitors are welcome and there is a Grape Festival organized by Casa Madero in Parras every August.

### Cheverny/Tradición

These are the two brand-names of the Mexican brandies made for Martell, the French cognac house. They are produced near San Juan del Rio from Ugni Blanc grapes in Martell's own 323 hectares (800 acres) of vineyards that were first planted in 1965.

### Presidente

This is the Domecq brand of grape brandy that currently sells around five million cases every year, making it top-seller in Mexico, South America and the world.

Not content with that degree of product-distribution, the Domecq company also owns the third-ranked brand, Don Pedro, which adds another two million cases to the overall sales total.

The Domecq soleras are located in a large complex in the Los Reyes area of Mexico City. Much of the plant is laid out with visitors in mind, as with the glass-fronted barrels that let you see the brandy during its ageing period.

### PRESIDENTE

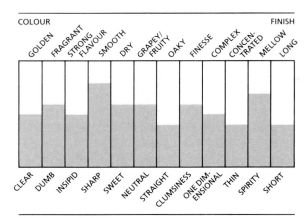

## Viejo Vergel

The second-ranking brand in Mexico's blockbusting top three, accounting for about four million cases a year. The company was set up in 1943 when a local cotton-planter, Luís Garza, diversified into brandy and wine. Much of the brandy is distilled at Aguascalientes, but the company has an old winery and distillery near Gómez Palacio with extraordinary underground cellars; they are vaulted like great gothic crypts and supported by splendid marble pillars.

Visitors are welcome.

# PERU

## OCUCAJE

The main brand of pisco brandy from the wine-growing area of Ica, Peru, where it may well have originated in the 17th century. The brandy is full and zesty with good Moscatel fragrance and grapey flavour. It bears some resemblance to the artisanal Moscato grappa of northern Italy.

*Port grapes from its own Quintas vineyards are used to produce Calem's bagaceira.*

The pisco name is said to derive from the local Indian tribe who first made the earthenware pots in which the spirit was stored. The town of Pisco along the coast was once the port to the area, from which exports of the brandy would initially have gone.

Ocucaje distil from Moscatel – close family to the grape that yields Italy's aromatic Asti Spumante wine – but there are a number of other eligible grapes for making the spirit. Pisco should be distilled in pot-stills from wine but much of it is also made from pomace, or both. Most of it is drunk young but a tiny amount is aged in Chile, where good pisco is also made.

Ica is a most interesting location. The valley is a verdant break in the Peruvian coastal desert and not far from the famous drawings on the desert floor at Nazca. Another pre-Columbian land-drawing – the giant candelabrum of the Andes that is scoured out of a sloping sand-hill on the Paracas peninsula – lies west of Pisco itself.

### OCUCAJE MOSCATEL PISCO DE ICA

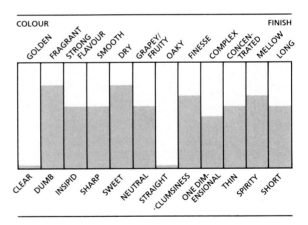

# PORTUGAL

Grape brandy in Portugal is called *aguardente* (cf. *aguardiente de orujo* in Spain which is pomace brandy) and *bagaceira* is the Portuguese name for pomace spirit. Much less brandy is made in Portugal in relation to its volume of wine production than in other countries – perhaps 10–12 million litres a year.

The well-known Vinho Verde wine from the north of the country is ideal for distillation because of its high acidity (*verde* means 'green' in the sense of 'unripe'). Portugal's brandies are similar in style to those of Spain but are slightly drier. Many have a richness, however, that comes from being matured in casks that have been used for port. They are generally very smooth in finish, since most of the distillation is done in continuous stills.

## Calem

Famous port house's brand-name that is also used for their three-year-old brandy (aguardente) and a year-old bagaçeira that is made from port grapes. Ageing is carried out in Memel and Portuguese oak casks, most of which have formerly held port.

Calem has been family-owned since 1859 and has always been a port specialist. It owns vineyards of port grapes so it distils its own bagaçeira after each vintage. As regards aguardente, it buys in distillate, ages it and blends it – the processes which are the most formative part of making good brandy.

The winemaker at Calem is an Englishman, Jeremy Bull; there are quite a few of them around in the port trade, and there always have been. Calem exports brandy to the Far East, Australasia, Canada and the United States. With the growing interest in grappa in the latter, the company is making plans to launch its bagaçeira on that market.

Visitors to the port lodges in Vila Nova de Gaia are always welcome.

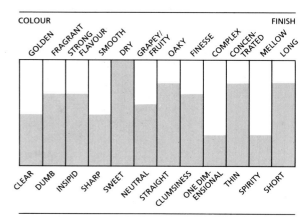

### CALEM AGUARDENTE

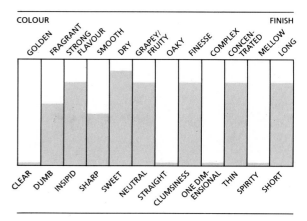

### CALEM BAGACEIRA

*The Calem vineyard at São Martinho de Anta. Calem plans to expand its international market for bagaceira.*

## Dalva/Douro fathers

Three pot-still brandies that are kept and aged for as long as it takes to get them absolutely right; there are no short cuts.

The VSOP, so described, must be just about the oldest in the world. The Douro Fathers is the brand name used for the five-year-old exported to New Zealand, a brandy that is soft, grapey and quite sweet.

The Dalva VO is 12-years-old and shows natural sweet woodiness and zesty length of flavour. Dalva VSOP is all of 30-years-old with just about everything fully developed – it is full-bodied, complex, fragrant and long in finish, but still with good spirit structure. The brandies are aged in oak casks that have held port, the main business of the da Silvas family, hence the richness of the house-style.

The company has been in business since 1862 as a producer of port and brandy, and its role today regarding the brandies is to blend and age them.

## DOURO FATHERS 5 YEARS-OLD

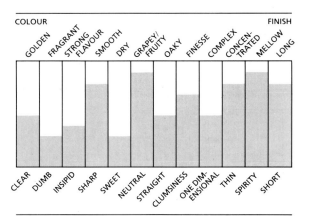

## DALVA VSOP 30 YEARS-OLD

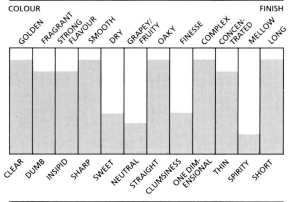

## DALVA 12 YEARS-OLD

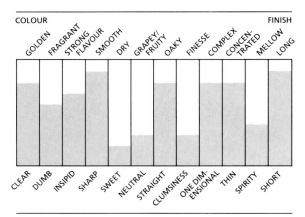

# TUNISIA

## Soleil

One of the better-known brands of *boukha*, the Arab name for *eau-de-vie de figues*, fig brandy. Soleil is produced at the F. Habib distillery in Tunis. It is water-white and not aged, with a light roundness that comes from continuous distillation. Soleil – as with all the better types of boukha – is wholly dry and restrained, with a quite concentrated aroma of the fruit; the sloppier styles are sweeter and uncomfortably close in character to syrup of figs.

## SOLEIL BOUKHA

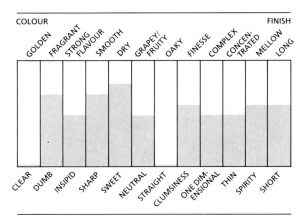

# UNITED KINGDOM

## Somerset Royal

A cider brandy from Royal Somerset apples grown entirely in the county of Somerset in south-west England. The style is clean, dry and authentic in its

*Even smaller distillers will employ their own cooper to repair and maintain their barrel stock.*

## SOMERSET ROYAL

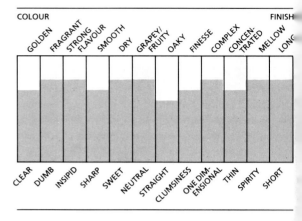

| | COLOUR | | | | | | | | | | | | FINISH |
|---|---|---|---|---|---|---|---|---|---|---|---|---|---|
| | GOLDEN | FRAGRANT | STRONG FLAVOUR | SMOOTH | DRY | GRAPEY/ FRUITY | OAKY | FINESSE | COMPLEX | CONCEN- TRATED | MELLOW | LONG | |
| | CLEAR | DUMB | INSIPID | SHARP | SWEET | NEUTRAL | STRAIGHT | CLUMSINESS | ONE DIM- ENSIONAL | THIN | SPIRITY | SHORT | |

apple aromas and flavour, with a full tannin presence. The technique is based on that of Calvados in France, just across the English Channel from the distillery, and indeed the still was brought over from there.

Continuous distillation is an option in all but one of the Calvados zones, and this is the process that has been adopted for making Somerset Royal. Ageing is in oak barrels for three years and the first vintage, 1987, emerged from bond in 1990 entirely pre-sold. Most of the 1988 that will be released in 1991 has also been allocated. As a unique, hand-made, single-distillery brandy it costs about the same as a 15-year-old armagnac or one of the better VSOP cognacs.

The brandy is in highly successful commercial production today only because the owner took on the British Customs and dug in until he got permission to run a full working distillery. Cider-distillation was outlawed in England 200 years ago in favour of cereal spirits and the only cider brandy made up to 1987 was in two museum stills in the west of England grouchily sanctioned by the Customs.

One was run by Bertram Bulmer, a doyen of the famous English cider-making dynasty, in Hereford, and the other was at a country estate belonging to the Clive-Ponsonby-Fane family at Brympton d'Evercy in Somerset. Julian Temperley was the distiller there for a short while. A cider-maker at Martock, in Somerset, he had spent some time going back and forth to Calvados to learn how to distil.

The French were very helpful and even sold him a second-hand still. When he came back with it, even with the correct paperwork, Customs took 12 hours to let him through. In all it took him 10 years of negotiation to get his licence.

### Bristol Brandy Company

This is not a producer of brandy but a specialist business that deals in high-quality spirits. Its commercial scope is so much in tune with the broad subject-matter of this book that it seems worth drawing the attention of readers to it — particularly since it despatches orders to customers on request. Sales are by unbroken case-minimum.

It supplies early-landed cognacs in bottle and in cask (e.g. Delamain 1987 Grande Champagne) and there are many interesting single-bottle opportunities, like Hine 1904 Grande Champagne. There are also single-domaine armagnacs from a wide range of producers in six-bottle cases, fruit eaux-de-vie from Switzerland, vintage calvados, fines and marcs de Bourgogne and French plum brandy; the choice is outstanding.

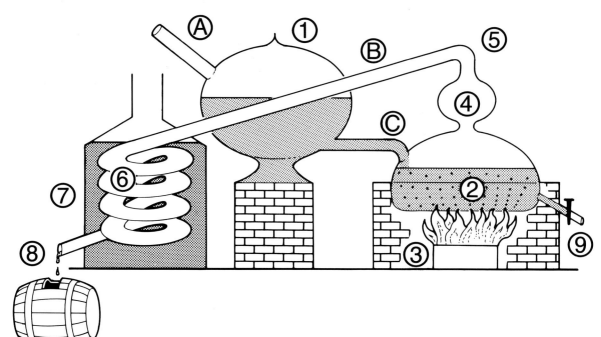

## POT-STILL DISTILLATION IN COGNAC

1 Chauffe-vin (wine-heater)
2 Chaudière (pot still)
3 Fire
4 Chapiteau (still-head)
5 Col de cygne (swan-neck)

6 Serpentin (cooking worm)
7 Cold-water tank
8 Spirit collected
9 Waste tap

The process of distilling cognac exemplifies the broad principles of pot-still spirit-production around the world:

Wine is run into the chauffe-vin (1) at A and is pre-heated by the boiled-off vapours already coming along pipe B from the still. In separate batches, the warmed wine is fed into the pot shaped still (2) at C and is eventually boiled by the heat-source (3). In Cognac this must be a naked-flame fire, traditionally burning wood but nowadays usually coal or gas. The first evaporation to come off is that of the alcohol because it has a lower boiling point than water. These vapours collect in the chapiteau (4), pass over the col de cygne (5) at the top of the still and pass along pipe B. As they pass through the chauffe-vin, the hot vapours are partly cooled by the cold wine stored there for the next distillation and are finally condensed by the serpentin (6) which lies in a tank of cold water (7). Spirit is collected at (8) and separated into heads, heart and tails (see text). Water left in the still is run off at (9) before the next distillation run. This distilling operation is carried out twice to make each batch of spirit. The first distillation is called the brouillis and reaches a strength of 25-30% abv; the second – the bonne chauffe – usually produces the final spirit at a strength of 70% abv. Very rarely spirit is triple-distilled to high strength and a high degree of refinement. NB: The chauffe-vin, although widely used, is optional and some important distillers prefer not to use one.

# BIBLIOGRAPHY

Robert Delamain. 1937. *Histoire du Cognac.* Editions Stock (Delamain et Boutelleau, Paris, 1935).

Nicholas Faith. 1987. *Cognac and Other Brandies — Pocket Guide.* Mitchell Beazley.

James Long. 1983: *Companion to Cognac and Other Brandies.* Century.

Luigi Papo. 1987. *Italian Brandy.* Alinari, Florence.

Cyril Ray. 1985. *Cognac.* Harrap.

J. and G. Samalens. (J. Goolden, ed.) 1983. *Armagnac.* Christies.

# GLOSSARY

These are the main terms used in brandy-making. Various technical terms are also included in the index.

| | |
|---|---|
| **abv** | alcohol by volume. The quantity of alcohol present in a spirit expressed as a percentage. Most brandy is 38–43% abv. Note that abv 40% = UK Proof 70% = US Proof 80%. |
| **Aguardente** | Portuguese term for grape brandy (= 'burning water'). |
| **Aguardiente de orujo** | Spanish term for pomace brandy. |
| **Alambic Armagnacais** | Special form of continuous still, traditional in the Armagnac region. |
| **Alambic Charentais/ Cognaçais** | Pot-still traditional to brandy-making in Cognac/the Charentes. |
| **Alquitara** | Name given to a pot-still and its distillate in Spain. |
| **Alter** | *see* Weinbrand. |
| **Bagaceira** | Portuguese term for pomace brandy. |
| **Boisé** | Essence made from oak chips steeped in spirit or brandy and added to maturing brandy to supplement tannin level and/or enhance woody aroma. |
| **Bonne Chauffe** | French term for second and (usually) final distillation to make brandy spirit. |
| **Bouilleur** | Professional distiller in France who usually produces spirit for the large brand-owning firms. |
| **Brandewijn** | Dutch term (meaning 'burnt wine') for brandy and probably the origin of the word. |
| **Brouillis** | French term for the first of two distillations in the process of making brandy spirit. |
| **Calandre** | Type of chambered still used to make some marc and fine. |
| **Chai** | Storage area above ground (cf. cave which is a cellar) for barrels of brandy (French). |
| **Chapiteau** | Top of a pot-still where the spirit vapour is channelled off to condense. |
| **Chaudière** | Reservoir in still where the wine is boiled off during the distillation process. |
| **Chauffe-vin** | An optional tank in a still which utilises the heat from the vapour pipe to preheat the wine about to be distilled (French, 'wine-heater'). |
| **Coffey still** | Type of continuous still developed by Aeneas Coffey, a Dublin excise officer, in 1830. |
| **Col de cygne** | French for 'swan-neck', the pipe that carries the vapour from the still to the condenser. |
| **Congeners** | The flavouring elements carried over in distillation from the wine into the brandy. Highly-refined spirit lacks these. |
| **Continuous still** | Apparatus which distils a continuous flow of wine without interruption. Usually used for high-strength distillation which renders smooth but featureless spirit. |
| **Fine** | Grape brandy from delimited zones in France other than Cognac, Armagnac or Calvados; also, general term to denote a good-quality brandy. |
| **Heads** | The unsavoury initial spirit that comes over from a pot-still and which is rejected. |

| Heart | The wholesome middle portion or 'cut' in a distillation run that follows the heads and is collected as good spirit. |
|---|---|
| Holandas | Spanish spirit of 70% abv maximum with good congener content. Formerly for the Dutch market. |
| Lees | The name given to the debris left in a vat after grape-juice has fermented into wine. |
| Limousin | The name of the forest near Limoges, in France, which yields oak wood that is widely used for making the casks in which brandy is aged. |
| Rancio | A sought-after aroma characteristic, finely balanced between mellowness and decay, that is associated with very old, distinguished brandy. |
| Serpentin | The French word for the 'snake-like' coil of cooling pipe that is immersed in cold water to condense the vapours from the still into spirit. Also known as a worm. |
| Straight | Term for California brandy that has not had flavouring enhancers like prune juice or 'sherry' added to it. |
| Tails | The final part of a distillation run from a pot-still that is mainly water and thus rejected. |
| Tronçais | Important French oak forest, like Limousin (q.v.), from which wood is obtained to make maturation casks for brandy spirit. |
| Uralt | *See* Weinbrand. |
| Vin viné | Semi-fortified wine used, as in Germany, for brandy-distillation. |
| Weinbrand | German word for grape brandy. 'Alter' or 'Uralt' used in conjunction with it indicates that a brandy has been aged in wood for at least a year. |
| Vieux Faibles | Mixture of brandy and distilled water used to reduce the strength of matured cask brandy without disturbing its 'togetherness'. |

## *METRIC UNITS*

| Metric unit | | USA equivalent | UK equivalent |
|---|---|---|---|
| 1 litre | (l) | = 1.057 quarts | = 1.75 pints |
| 1 hectolitre | (hl) | = 105.7 quarts | = 175 pints |
| 1 kilometre | (km) | = 0.62 mile | (US and UK) |
| 1 hectare | (ha) | = 2.47 acres | (US and UK) |
| 1 kilogram | (kg) | = 2.2046 lb | (US and UK) |

# Index

# *PICTURE CREDITS*